ON MY
HONOUR

ON MY HONOUR

ONE MAN'S LIFELONG STRUGGLE TO CLEAR HIS NAME

―――➤●◄―――

BRENDON K. COLVERT

MERCIER PRESS

IRISH PUBLISHER – IRISH STORY

MERCIER PRESS

Cork

www.mercierpress.ie

© Text: Brendon K. Colvert, 2011

© Foreword: Conor Brady, 2011

ISBN: 978 1 85635 756 2

10 9 8 7 6 5 4 3 2 1

A CIP record for this title is available from the British Library

Printed and bound in the EU.

CONTENTS

ACKNOWLEDGEMENTS

Along the tedious way to William Geary's vindication, various people lent support to his claims for justice, and others helped to prove his innocence beyond doubt. It is not possible, of course, to place a measure on the goodwill or significance of each person's assistance; his godson Judge John P. Collins of the Supreme Court of the State of New York may, however, be described as the slingshot that toppled Goliath.

Amongst those most worthy of mention would be: Seán Ó Brosnacháin, OC 'F' Coy, 3 Battalion West Limerick Brigade (Old IRA); Sergeant John Gallagher, Garda Síochána, registration number 2225; Donagh O'Brien, TD, Limerick; Fr Thomas K. Carroll, Longford; Valerie Kelly, research officer, the Labour Party; Frank Prendergast, TD, the Labour Party; the Reverend Donald K. O'Callaghan, Order of Carmelites; John Vincent Moran, journalist; Dr Henry O. Teltscher, Grapho Diagnostic; Nat Laurendi, Certified Polygraphist, NYPD 1951–75; Conor Brady, editor, *The Irish Times*; Professor Dermot Walsh, director of the Centre for Criminal Justice, University of Limerick; Margaret Ward, journalist, *The Irish Times*; Mark Hennessy, political correspondent, *Irish Examiner*; Ron Kirwan, *Limerick Leader*; Nollaig Ó Gadhra, Iriseoir, Luimneach; Bertie Ahern, Taoiseach; John O'Donoghue, TD, Minister for

Justice; James B. Hill, Garda Síochána, spouse of Marie (née Drake), a cousin of William Geary; Tim Leahy, former garda superintendent at Kilrush; and Professor James (Jim) Gillogly and Dr Thomas Mahon, authors of *Decoding the IRA*.

Valuable assistance in procuring photographs and records was provided by the Garda Museum, Dublin Castle; Jim Herlihy, genealogist; Superintendent Tim Leahy, ret.; John Collins, Riverdale, NY; Fr Gerard Carroll, Longford; Edward Nolan, Mullingar; Joan Kennedy, Thurles; Conor Brady, Dublin; Margaret Ward, Dublin; National Archives, Bishop Street, Dublin 8; Garda Commissioner Fachtna Murphy; the Taoiseach's Office; the Department of Justice, Equality and Law Reform; Peter Beirne, archivist, Clare County Library, Ennis; *Garda Review* magazine; and the electoral offices of Bertie Ahern, TD, and John O'Donoghue, TD.

I gratefully acknowledge the assistance of my dear brother Dominic.

FOREWORD

William Geary, the remarkable man who is the subject of this book, lived a full and accomplished life, ultimately achieving his cherished goal of clearing his name and redeeming his honour. But he had to struggle for that success against a background of adversity and injustice that would surely have broken a lesser individual. His campaign to secure his good name endured for almost seventy years from the fateful day in 1928 when he was summarily dismissed from his superintendency in the Garda Síochána and effectively forced into exile.

The story told here by Brendon Colvert, himself a distinguished former member of the gardaí, is not merely that of an injustice done in the early years of the Irish state and then consigned to history. It is a moving narrative of official cowardice and obfuscation, maintained over decades, as an ageing man sought to bring out the truth behind the original travesty.

I am probably the only person alive who discussed the events narrated here with the two principals of the tale: William Geary himself and David Neligan, the head of the gardaí's crime branch from 1922 until 1932 when he was removed by the Fianna Fáil government of Eamon de Valera. In 1973–1974 when researching my postgraduate thesis at UCD, I conducted a series of interviews with David Neligan at his home in Dublin.

Thirty years later, while a visiting professor at John Jay College at the City University of New York, I had the great pleasure of visiting William Geary at his home in the Borough of Queens.

I have two overriding impressions of those encounters. I recall the thread of regret and sorrow that ran through David Neligan's recollections. And I recall the remarkable absence of bitterness in William Geary's narrative of his life. Recalling my discussions with Neligan, I feel that in his heart he knew that William Geary had been wronged. Why then, one must ask, did he not come out and say so, all those years ago? I suspect that Neligan believed that, regardless of what he might say, the state would not admit to a mistake and that the wronged Geary would still have no justice. There were a great many things in David Neligan's career that he felt were best left unvisited and unexamined in his old age.

Much of the story of William Geary is in the public domain thanks to the work of former Superintendent Tim Leahy and *Irish Times* journalist Margaret Ward. Brendon Colvert's coup is in securing the full texts of the documents that effectively comprised the indictment of William Geary in 1928: the intelligence report prepared by Chief Superintendent Neligan for the then commissioner of the force, Eoin O'Duffy, and O'Duffy's report to the cabinet via the Minister for Justice, James Fitzgerald Kenney. These official documents are remarkable and, indeed, shocking for their lack of deductive rigour, their inaccuracies and, in places, their incoherence. In any open forum, such as a court of law, they would have been torn to shreds and their authors castigated. Mr Colvert's contribution in bringing these fully to light is not to be underestimated.

It must be deduced from Neligan's and O'Duffy's vehemence that they believed in Geary's guilt. Neither had any vested interest in identifying a security breach among the elite officer corps of the force which they themselves had built and developed, and of which O'Duffy, in particular, was very proud. The two men would have been, in some degree, compromised and diminished by such a thing.

There was some evidence against William Geary. But it was not tested, as it would be today. For example, although it was alleged that Geary had taken £100 from the Irish Republican Army (IRA) as a bribe, it seems that no attempt was made to locate evidence of any such payment in his bank account or anywhere else. It has to be assumed that the evidence was contrived or planted and that William Geary was 'set up'. In all probability that was the work of the local IRA which was headed by a particularly resourceful and wily officer called T. J. Ryan. By odd coincidence, Ryan (like William Geary) had also served as a Marconi officer with the merchant navy.

It may seem bizarre at this remove that the IRA would have gone to such elaborate lengths to discredit the police superintendent in what was, after all, a remote and insignificant district. Had they sought to discredit O'Duffy or Neligan or some of the influential headquarters staff that might have made more strategic sense. In reality, however, this rather obscure district in the west of Ireland had a particular significance for the IRA and those who still believed they could bring down the

Treaty of 1921 by force of arms. Long after other parts of the country had been pacified, West Clare continued to be a place where violence was commonplace, where firearms were available to young men who were prepared to use them and where the new state was seen as vulnerable.

Already a uniformed garda, Tom Dowling, had been killed in 1925 in North Clare, near Fanore (although his death was at the hands of ordinary criminals rather than the IRA); in 1929 a detective officer, Tadgh O'Sullivan, had been killed at Tullycrine. Jurors and witnesses in cases taken against suspected IRA members had been intimidated, shot at and had their properties destroyed. One potential witness in West Clare had disappeared and was believed to have been murdered.

Taking down the district police chief would have been considered a worthwhile prize. The local superintendent was effectively the state's man in a district. The IRA knew that if the men in this role could be neutralised it would represent a significant achievement for their aims of rolling back the state's authority. Two years later, the IRA in Tipperary, adjoining County Clare, killed the local superintendent, Seán Curtin, because he had become 'over-zealous' in his work.

It is also possible that William Geary had consciously moved into dangerous waters in his work in Clare. It may well have been that he had endeavoured to develop intelligence links with the IRA. Many local superintendents did, and it was frequently a rich source of useful intelligence to the authorities. Perhaps the local IRA felt he knew too much or perhaps he had persuaded some local IRA members to be 'of assistance' to the police. We shall probably never know the truth about these possibilities. All of the members of the West Clare IRA of the period are long dead (Ryan died in 1962) and, as far as we know, no documents or memoirs relevant to the William Geary case have survived.

Insofar as the term 'happy ending' may have any meaning, however, the story of William Geary had one. He died in 2004, aged 105, content and proud that his name had been cleared and that he had been acclaimed by the state and by the police force that had condemned him so many decades before. It is a pity that his health was such that he was unable to return to Ireland. The commissioner of the Garda Síochána in 2004, Patrick Byrne, offered to fête him at the depot headquarters and to honour him in the old officers' mess that had been his 'prison' while awaiting his fate in 1928.

It is my understanding that Brendon Colvert's book is to be launched in the old 'mess' at the Phoenix Park Depot. That will be fitting. It is an ancient building, dating from the era of the Irish constabulary. It is filled with history and memories and it is not difficult to imagine the shades of long-gone policemen among its fine rooms and corridors. No doubt, if they were there, they would raise a hearty cheer to see one of their own triumph, finally, against the injustice of the system.

Conor Brady
25 November 2010

INTRODUCTION

My introduction to the William Geary story was through a feature I published in May 1997 in a Jubilee Edition of the *IPA Journal* (the journal of the International Police Association). To salute the surviving original members of the Garda Síochána I elicited their names from what seemed to be the most reliable source and published details of the ten known survivors. Then in October 2002, as editor of the *IPA Journal*, with the kind permission of the Garda Síochána Retired Members Association (GSRMA), I produced another feature, titled 'Charlie Clarke' – the name of the man who, by this time, was reputed to be the sole surviving original member of the Garda Síochána. Soon afterwards I received a letter, dated 22 October 2002, from James B. Hill. He informed me:

> While on holiday in the US recently my wife and I visited her cousin William Geary, another original member of an Garda Síochána. As has been well documented elsewhere he joined in May 1922, Registration Number 938, and in 1928 while serving as a Superintendent in Kilrush, Co. Clare, he was sacked for allegedly taking a bribe. This resulted in his exile to New York and a campaign by him for over seventy years to clear his name.
>
> This had a positive outcome in April 1999 when the

Government considered it reasonable that Mr Geary should have the 'impediment to the future enjoyment of his good name and reputation lifted'. He was granted a lump sum and a pension equivalent to that of a Superintendent retiring after completing full service.

I am glad to report that he is hale and hearty and living on his own. He is very active and is looking forward to celebrating his 104th birthday next February.[1]

This letter whetted my appetite for more information. It led to the discovery of new and fascinating facts about William Geary and to his story being recounted here.

To evaluate the evidence, I first examined the records in the Garda Museum in Dublin Castle. Then the task of obtaining relevant information from the Irish government began. File S 9051 in the National Archives was reputed to contain all the relevant information that led to William Geary's dismissal in the first instance. Persistent efforts – on 12 November, 15 November and 7 December in 2007 – to view this file failed.

On 27 May 2009 I wrote to the director of the National Archives and was advised to contact the certifying officer at the Department of the Taoiseach; this I did on 5 June 2009. Subsequently, having sent a registered letter of request on 30 June 2009, I was informed that my request had been forwarded to the designated consenting officer. On 6 August 2009 John Kennedy, of the office of the secretary general, wrote to me and enclosed a copy of another file (S 26143/1) and some information from file S 9051. The vital evidence against William Geary was reduced to a limp file showing poor quality copies of documents at the point of illegibility. This information from the prime minister's office was the end of the line as far as cooperation by that state department was concerned.

I had better luck when I was permitted to examine the Geary files in the Department of Justice on 12 November 2009. To my amazement, I held in my hand the photograph of the original letter from the Irish Republican Army (IRA) chief in County Clare to the director of intelligence in Dublin, which had been intercepted and which formed the basis for William Geary's dismissal.

Readers will see parallels in William Geary's story with that of Alfred Dreyfus, a Jewish French Army captain, falsely accused in 1894 of selling secrets to the Germans. He was given a dishonourable discharge and sentenced to life imprisonment on Devil's Island off the coast of French Guiana. Through the intervention of the novelist, playwright and journalist Émile Zola, he was retried in 1899 and given a pardon by President Émile Loubet. In 1906 he was exonerated and reinstated with the rank of major and acclaimed an *Officier du Légion d'Honneur*; thus ended Dreyfus' twelve-year fight against anti-Semitism. In William Geary's case, we see a heroic, seventy-year struggle against the forces nurtured by an internecine war and by bureaucratic bungling. Shakespeare surely knew how those like Dreyfus and Geary feel:

Who steals my purse steals trash; 'tis something, nothing;
'Twas mine, 'tis his and has been a slave to thousands;

But he that filches from me my good name
Robs me of that which not enriches him,
And makes me poor indeed.[2]

I believe that people who read William Geary's story will find, with some amazement, that it took an inordinate amount of time for successive Irish governments to recognise the meaning of natural justice and to act on that recognition.

1

Rural Roots

William Geary was born before the end of the nineteenth century, the second son in what would become a family of eight children. He first saw the light of day on 28 February 1899 in the old, thatched, two-storey Cloonee Cottage near Ballyagran, County Limerick. Ballyagran was a small rural village with three public houses, a church, a post office, a grocery store, a tailor, a carpenter, a blacksmith and a stonemason to serve the community.

His father Patrick was what would be termed a 'gentleman farmer', with ninety-two acres of good land for mixed farming. The family milked twenty-eight cows, made butter, killed two pigs each year and ground their own wheat to make bread. They employed a man to plough, mind stock and mow the meadows. In the house, a housemaid and a nanny assisted William's mother Helen. On Sundays at mass they sat in a family-designated pew in the parish church. And it is reported that each year they paid the substantial sum of £3 into the collections.

In William's early days, Ireland was part of the British Empire, on which 'the sun never set' – it stretched across Africa,

Canada, the Middle East, India, Australia and New Zealand. Knowledge of the outside world in the village in the early days of the twentieth century was concerned to a great extent with the interests of the Empire.

During the period in which William went from being a babe in arms to finishing primary school and being a useful farmhand, the American dollar went on the gold standard; the Abbey Theatre opened in Dublin; Queen Victoria died; Pope Leo XIII died; the great Italian tenor Enrico Caruso made his first recording; aspirin went on sale; the one-minute San Francisco earthquake killed at least 700 people; Orville and Wilbur Wright took flight; Robert Peary reached the North Pole; Louis Blériot flew the English Channel; Guglielmo Marconi won the Nobel Prize in Physics for his development of wireless telegraphy; Roald Amundsen reached the South Pole; the *Titanic* sank; the Panama Canal was opened; chlorine gas was used at Ypres in the First World War; the *Lusitania* was torpedoed; the 1916 Rebellion took place in Dublin; the first air service was established between London and Paris; and John Alcock and Arthur Whitten Brown flew the Atlantic. All of these events were in the news headlines and topics of adult conversation that would have been of interest to William's eager young mind.

But the wider culture, so often caught up with the concerns of the Empire, clashed with Celtic, tribal and religious ideals prevalent among William's family and friends. There was, in fact, a colonial imposition, resented for its history of suppression of freedom of conscience and for economic aggression. The family home had originally been built as a 'garrison' house with steel bars protecting its windows from possible assault by the local Irish. The Geary family, comfortable with their Irishness, lived in it and tended its garden. The young man lived a peaceful rural life but later casually joined the rebel Volunteers in the fight for Irish freedom. The drive for tranquillity in the civic order versus cultural and political freedom was part of his maturing process.

The British hegemony can be seen in the prohibition of the Irish language from the primary school curriculum. However, the conflict with this hegemony can be seen in the fact that the principal at Ballyagran National School, Mr Quill, an Irish nationalist, taught the language for half an hour each day, before official lessons began, to those who wished to learn it. Irish language tests were held annually in Limerick. Ballyagran National School won the competition on three occasions and the victory shield was displayed prominently in the school.

William's father died in 1907 and responsibility for farm work shifted to his widow and his young sons as they matured. It encouraged family cohesion and the fatherly interest of his Uncle Michael, who owned a nearby farm.

William left the village primary school in 1914 when fifteen years old and continued his work on the farm, weeding, milking, cleaning stables and the myriad tasks associated with mixed farming. At sixteen he was selling calves at Dromcollogher fair. The passage of his life was marked only by seasonal changes, and when he was not hard at work, he found time to be a keen observer of the flora and fauna of his surroundings. As a centenarian he was able to describe with perfect recall the names and descriptions of more than twenty-five wild birds that frequented the fields and waterways around Ballyagran when he was growing up; he spoke about the arrival of migratory birds and the lore associated with their movements. (The acuity and reliability of William's memory, as shown in this recall, are also displayed in his later correspondence – particularly that with politicians, whereby he could confound them as they sought to confuse him about official records. His 1999 letter containing an analysis of the damning report on him by Chief Superintendent David Neligan in 1928 is an example.)[1]

During William's formative years in Ballyagran, he learned to be observant, dutiful, diligent, generous and honest; these traits characterised this gentleman in success and failure throughout his long life. The years encompassed by his youthful experiences made him adaptable and self-confident. It was this character that was to fortify him for life later in the hardscrabble of the New World.

2

THE YOUNG MAN

William Geary often marvelled at how significant events in his life came about by the chance intervention of others. In 1919, at age twenty, he was still working on the family farm. He was doing some gardening when his uncle approached him and asked if he would like to become a radio officer, telling him that he would pay the training fees. William accepted with alacrity; no doubt the possibility of world travel, a smart uniform and good pay was very alluring. He took leave of the farm and his family. First he went by pony and trap to Newcastle West railway station. From there his train passed through Listowel, Ardfert, Tralee and Farranfore, and then along the spectacularly scenic route via tunnels and viaducts in the Kerry mountains to the Atlantic Ocean.

William trained at the Atlantic Wireless School in Caherciveen, County Kerry. By August of 1919, he had obtained a First Class Certificate of Proficiency.[1] In that same month he sailed as an officer aboard the coal-fired tramp steamer SS *City of Birmingham*. As a ship's officer, he experienced a life quite different from that of a farm worker: he wore a smart uniform and had a batman to shine shoes, polish buttons, serve at table, and do the laundry.

His first and only voyage took him to London, Cape Town, Durban, Portuguese East Africa, Philadelphia, New York, Gibraltar, Suez, Bombay, Madras, Calcutta, Colombo, Ceylon, back to London and then to Liverpool. On 21 January 1921 he arrived in Liverpool, where he signed off – and where, due to lack of trade and shipping, his appointment was terminated.

He went home to Cloonee Cottage and resumed life on the farm. The 'Troubles', as the rebellion against British authority was known, were in full swing. After the failure of more conventional warfare in the 1916 uprising, the Irish Volunteers had perfected guerrilla warfare whereby mobile Volunteers whose logistics depended on local support would strike the enemy and then fade from the scene.

The British government, faced with protracted bloody conflict and with international disapproval of the increasingly terrorist tactics it employed, sought a truce with the Irish rebels in 1921. The result was a peace treaty satisfactory to no one: the Anglo-Irish Treaty signed on 6 December 1921. The Irish Free State was established on 6 December 1922 under this Treaty. Article 1 of the Constitution declared: 'The Irish Free State (otherwise hereinafter called or sometimes called Saorstát Éireann) is a co-equal member of the Community of Nations forming the British Commonwealth of Nations.'[2] All laws enacted by the Executive Council required the 'assent' of the King of England; members of the Irish parliament were obliged to take an oath of allegiance to King George V and to his heirs and successors. Northern Ireland was permitted to opt out of the Irish Free State.

As the imposed subservience to the British crown was unacceptable to those who were against the Treaty, the Irish rebels split into 'Free State' and 'anti-Treaty' factions, which fought for control of the country and public opinion. The members of the IRA who accepted the Treaty were deemed to have broken their sacred oath and reneged on their allegiance to Dáil Éireann (the Irish parliament), an elected assembly established in 1919, which had recognised the Volunteers as its legitimate army. The Free State faction took up the reins of government in Dublin. The anti-Treaty faction, known as the IRA, fought to establish a republic, but was soon outgunned. With the death of the republican chief of staff, General Liam Lynch, in April 1923, a ceasefire was declared, but the passions released by fratricidal warfare and the resulting cycle of atrocities and reprisals by both sides left a bitter legacy. Violence continued and the political divide affected the populace for generations. Indeed, in the twenty-first century two of the main political parties in the Republic of Ireland are the direct descendants of the opposing sides in this Civil War.

With the ending of William's career as a radio officer in 1921, he joined the Volunteers when he returned home to Ballyagran: 'the troubles persisted, the only activity in the locality was the training of the Volunteers. I thought it was normal, everybody was in the Volunteers. My captain was John Bresnihan, all we had was broomsticks, I showed them how to form fours, present arms and salute. That was about it.'[3]

William's work at home continued. He took care of the farming odd jobs, including the fetching of water. Water for house cleansing was collected in a large tank supplied from the roof of the barn, but water for cooking and personal consumption had to be brought from a well known as 'Ellen's well', about 150 metres from the house. One day William's mother asked him to fetch a bucket of water from the well. On the way there he encountered Jim Walsh, a neighbour, who suggested to William that he should join the Civic Guard, the new Irish police force established in 1922. Here was another moment of serendipity that changed the course of William's life – it was the impetus for an eventful career.

3

A WAR BETWEEN BROTHERS

The evils of war are multiplied in civil conflicts, and during the Civil War Irish men who had recently enjoyed the fellowship of comrades-in-arms now became mortal enemies. Nothing could condone the crimes committed by desperate adversaries on both sides in this war. In an effort to force a surrender by the anti-Treaty 'irregulars', the Free State government introduced a policy of executing IRA prisoners by simply charging them, at a military court martial, with bearing arms against the state; the government troops also summarily killed captured anti-Treaty IRA men before they even got to a court martial. There is a special repulsiveness about the institutional killing of helpless prisoners when the heat of battle has passed.

In reprisal, the republican chief of staff, General Liam Lynch, played a role in the bitterness of the Civil War by issuing orders against the Provisional Government on 30 November 1922: 'All members of the Provisional "Parliament" who were present and voted for the Murder Bill [setting up military courts with the power to impose a death penalty] will be shot at sight.' Another 'Captured Document' issued to 'O/C Battalion III' said:

The following will be shot at sight ... (a) all members who voted for Enemy Murder Bill; (b) officials of all rank; (c) members of senate in list A; (d) members of Murder Gang; (e) officials – civilians who order prisoners to be fired on; (f) those who torture prisoners ...[1]

This order sanctioned the killing of members of parliament, as well as senators and certain judges and newspaper editors, in reprisal for the National Army's killing of captured republicans. During these reprisals the republicans suffered badly, as did a number of innocent and unarmed bystanders. A number of sordid incidents involving the National Army – especially the killing of unarmed prisoners in Ballyseedy and Countess Bridge in Kerry – directly affected the people and led to a new direction whereby prisoners who died in custody in the Kerry Command were interred by the troops in the area where the death had taken place.

One of the best-known National Army figures in Kerry was David Neligan, a man who would play a leading part in the story of William Geary. Neligan had joined the Dublin Metropolitan Police (DMP) in 1917 and two years later was recruited into the political G Division. In 1920 his brother Maurice prevailed on him to resign, and he returned to Limerick. However, Michael Collins, the masterful head of IRA intelligence, persuaded him to rejoin and he was accepted back because his service record in the DMP had been very good. In these ruthless surroundings, Neligan undertook the very dangerous task of passing information to the IRA. In 1921 he was recruited into British intelligence and he became a very important mole for Collins in Dublin Castle. Double agent David Neligan, serving King George V, will long be remembered for his part in the assassination in one day of fourteen of the top British secret-service agents – the Cairo Gang, so called because they frequented Café Cairo – on 21 November 1920. This incident is made doubly memorable by the savage British revenge. That afternoon crown forces opened fire during a football match in a crowded Croke Park stadium in Dublin, killing one player and thirteen spectators.

After the truce between the British government and the Irish rebels in 1921, Neligan joined the National Army. In the early stages of the Civil War, on 31 July 1922, he sailed on the *Lady Wicklow* from Dublin as commandant with General Eoin O'Duffy and 450 men, landing in Fenit, County Kerry, on 2 August. Later, as chief of intelligence in the south, he acquired a reputation for cruelty and torture. Professor Dorothy Macardle noted: 'Interrogation by Neligan in Ballymullen Barracks was an ordeal under which reason might give way … The prisoner, in the usual practice, was first blindfolded, then his arms were tied to his sides, and the "interrogation" began.'[2]

But other instances of more lethal cruelty – which exemplify the deadly antagonisms of the Civil War – were brought to light: the killing of prisoners. On 5–6 March 1923 a landmine at Knocknagoshel killed five soldiers of the National Army. On 7 March, as a reprisal, nine prisoners – some with limbs broken from their interrogation – were taken to Ballyseedy, Tralee, where they were tied to a landmine and the landmine was exploded. Eight were killed. Against all odds Stephen Fuller escaped and the Curran family of Hanlon's Cross treated his wounds. On the same day four out of five prisoners who were bound to a landmine at Countess Bridge, Killarney, were killed. Again against all odds, Tadhg Coffey escaped. Five days later, on 12 March, five prisoners from the Workhouse, Caherciveen, were blown to pieces at Bahagh by the Free State forces. Before the explosion, bullets smashed the legs of the victims and none escaped. While it is not clear what role, if any, Neligan played in these extrajudicial killings, they highlight the climate of the times and the fact that in many cases army officers and government officials were implicated in behaviour outside the law and governing regulations.

At a meeting of Dáil Éireann on 17 April 1923 at Question Time, Tomás MacEoin, TD, asked the Minister for Defence whether he was now in a position to give an answer to a question asked on Tuesday 27 March relating to the death of eight prisoners at Ballyseedy, near Tralee, on 7 March. In a long reply General Richard Mulcahy stated that 'a Court of Enquiry was held at Tralee on the 7 April that had exonerated all of the military personnel concerned'.[3] However, from a cabinet meeting of 13 December 1923, some months after the end of the Civil War on 24 May 1923, we have the following report:

> The Minister of Home Affairs read a report which he had received from the Civic Guard in respect of a claim for compensation made by Maurice Riordan, Basilican, Waterville, County Kerry for the death of his son.

It was alleged in the claim that Riordan was taken out of Caherciveen Workhouse, where he was held prisoner by Officers of the Army and was murdered. The Civic Guard report was to the effect that this allegation was correct.

A copy of the report is to be sent to the Minister for Defence.[4]

Then on 22 January 1924, the following appears in the government records:

The memorandum submitted by the Ministry of Home Affairs regarding the death of William Riordan, an Irregular (anti-Treaty) prisoner at Caherciveen was considered.

It was decided that prima facia [sic] evidence of complicity in an attack against the State on the part of the applicant for compensation or the person in respect of whom compensation is claimed is a bar to the claim. The onus of preparing evidence in respect of any alleged excesses by the troops during the period of hostility rests upon the party who considers himself aggrieved.[5]

Even in the climate of the times, this ruling imposed an impossible burden on aggrieved persons and was a negation of civil rights.

After a cabinet meeting on 6 October 1924, the DMP and the Garda Síochána (the new name for the Civic Guard, introduced in August 1923), which up to that time had been separate police forces, were amalgamated. At the same time the Special Branch of armed detective units was formed under the leadership of Chief Superintendent David Neligan; this Special

Branch became what could be described as a parallel police force. The lawless practices of the Special Branch, and government involvement, can be gathered from official reports, for example:

> Pádraig Ó hÓgáin (An Clár) asked the Minister for Justice if he will state whether he has received from Kilrush Urban District Council a resolution demanding a sworn enquiry into the alleged misconduct of members of the Detective Division of the Garda Síochána in Clare, in connection with the arrest and detention of Thomas Breen, of Coolmeen, and T. J. Ryan, of Cranny, and whether, in view of such demand the sworn evidence submitted in substantiation of the charges, he will have such an enquiry instituted. Mr Fitzgerald Kenney, Minister for Justice, indicated 'I do not propose to take any further steps in the matter.'[6]

General Eoin O'Duffy was Commissioner of the Garda Síochána at the time when William Geary was dismissed. During the Civil War the youthful General O'Duffy was second only to Michael Collins in importance and he had commanded the rearguard action in Fenit, County Kerry – a tactical manoeuvre that greatly reduced the republicans' ability to organise. He was born on 20 October 1892 in Castleblayney, County Monaghan. Trained as an engineer, he became an assistant surveyor in County Monaghan and joined the Irish Volunteers in 1917. He was elected Ulster member of the Irish Republican Brotherhood (IRB) Supreme Council on 19 November of that year. During the War of Independence he commanded the historic sacking of Ballytrain Barracks on 14 February 1920. On 24 May 1921 he was elected as a Sinn Féin candidate to Dáil Éireann for County Monaghan and voted for the Treaty.[7]

In the National Army, O'Duffy was general officer commanding the Southern Command during the Civil War, becoming the youngest general in Europe. After the death of Michael Collins, he replaced General Richard Mulcahy as chief of staff. Having retired from the army, he was appointed Commissioner of the Civic Guard on 18 September 1922; while commissioner he was briefly recalled to service in the National Army as inspector-general of the defence forces following the 'Army Mutiny' in 1924. When the government had reduced the army by 30,000 men, this had been resisted by former members of Michael Collins' intelligence unit; eventually an army of 10,000 was established and brought under the control of the civil authority.

Even O'Duffy's most devoted admirers conceded that he was authoritarian and ruthless. Typical of his attitude is General Order Number 9 issued on 21 November 1922, in which he exhorts the unarmed Guards to resist all armed raids on barracks by anti-Treaty forces and not to surrender clothing, materials or records: 'The Civic Guard is largely composed of "column men" whose name for bravery and resource has become household words … If they are nothing more, they are Irishmen, and the Gael is not by nature a coward or a poltroon.'[8]

O'Duffy appears to have overlooked the fact that his 'column men' in the Civic Guard had been, a short while previously, comrades-in-arms of the very raiders who now attacked his force – men who were equally brave and determined. He regarded men as expendable to achieve his purpose.

O'Duffy, in moulding the Civic Guard to his requirements, issued eighteen General Orders between October 1922 and 20 December 1922. He also issued a publication signed 'Eoin Ua Dubhthaigh, Taoiseach, Coimisinéir' in 1924;[9] it was titled 'Standing General Orders' and contained thirty-two chapters of instructions which comprehensively covered all aspects of duties and responsibilities.

Oscar Traynor (1886–1963), a brigadier in the Irish Volunteers who took part in the Easter Rising of 1916, disliked O'Duffy intensely and once referred to him as 'a bloody liar'.[10] Traynor was elected to Dáil Éireann on both Sinn Féin and Fianna Fáil tickets and held several ministerial posts, including Defence and Justice.[11]

Apparently O'Duffy was an insecure person who courted popularity by telling people what he thought they wished to hear. Mary MacSwiney, the sister of Terence MacSwiney (the lord mayor of Cork, who had died on hunger strike in Brixton Prison), has been quoted as saying:

> He [O'Duffy] assured me that while Terry was in Brixton, he once heard one of his own men declare that Terry was committing suicide and that he should give up the hunger strike and he assured me that he had taken that man out, had given him half an hour and had him shot as a traitor.[12]

Historically, however, such an execution does not appear to have occurred.

Certain events following the Civil War established both

O'Duffy's continued idealism and also his overweening ambition and unpredictability. These events provide, too, a window on his character, and will therefore be considered briefly here, as O'Duffy will play an important role in subsequent chapters. As a leader he showed himself to be an organising genius, but as a commander it appears he had a predilection for high risks and, as is revealed in General Order Number 9, a disregard of the human cost of military or police operations.

In 1927 Eamon de Valera and his new party Fianna Fáil entered the Dáil. De Valera and O'Duffy were diametrically opposed politically, and following a general election in 1933 the Fianna Fáil government dismissed Commissioner O'Duffy. O'Duffy had appointed Inspector E. M. O'Connell as acting head of security when Chief Superintendent Neligan was moved to the Land Commission in 1932. Inspector O'Connell and Colonel Michael Hogan were arrested and charged with offences under the Official Secrets Act and the assumption was that O'Duffy had permitted information to be leaked to these men who were hostile to de Valera's party.

Many historians believe that the charging of O'Connell and Hogan was a mere contrivance because the accused officers were not convicted, but in an act of poetic justice it led to O'Duffy's dismissal from the police service on 27 February 1933 – just like his victim Superintendent William Geary some five years earlier. The ancient adage *filleann an feall ar an bhfeallaire* (treachery returns on the deceiver) is apt. De Valera explained his reason to the Dáil as follows: 'He [O'Duffy] was likely to be biased in his attitude because of past political affiliations.'[13] It became known that Commissioner O'Duffy had urged President William T. Cosgrave to resort to a military coup rather than turn over power to the incoming Fianna Fáil administration.

After his removal from office, O'Duffy established the Army Comrades Association, commonly referred to as 'the Blueshirts', which adopted a straight-arm salute and the slogan Hail O'Duffy! The newly created Cumann na nGaedheal Party appointed O'Duffy as its president in 1933, but distanced itself from his movement in 1934 as the Army Comrades Association was showing a taste for the trappings of fascism.

O'Duffy developed a cult of personality and by the time he entered politics his narcissism had become his greatest weakness; he even planned to have a mass march on Dáil Éireann to take over the government, which caused many defections. He went on to organise and lead an Irish Brigade and in 1936 led the 700-strong *Bandera Irlandesa* to Spain to fight alongside General Franco, despite the Irish government's prohibition of involvement in the Spanish Civil War. When the Irish Brigade sailed from Galway on 13 December 1936 aboard SS *Urundi* under the swastika flag, *The Irish Press* reported it under banner headlines: 'Liner Flies Emblem of German Nazis'. O'Duffy proclaimed himself the third most important man in Europe after Adolf Hitler and Benito Mussolini.

4

A Career in
the Garda Síochána

William Geary joined the police force on 2 May 1922 in
the new civic police headquarters in County Kildare.[1] The
new police force was mainly composed of many who had
been involved in the War of Independence as well as former
members of the Royal Irish Constabulary (RIC), farmers'
sons and tradesmen.

The title 'Civic Guard' continued from the time of establish-
ment until 1923. On 31 July 1923 the cabinet executive council
assembled and Deputy Thomas Johnson moved 'An Act to establish in Saorstát Éireann, and regulate a Police Force to be called
the Civic Guard.' Deputy Cathal O'Shannon proposed, 'I move
to substitute Garda Síochána for the words "Civic Guard" if
that would be in order.'[2] So the title of the force became Garda
Síochána na h-Éireann and the new force was modelled on the
Dublin Metropolitan Police; it was to be unarmed and headed
by a commissioner rather than a police chief.

Michael Joseph Staines was *ex officio* garda commissioner

from 2 February 1922 and was formally appointed first commissioner on 10 March 1922. He was at the same time an alderman of Dublin City and a deputy in the Irish government. Staines bravely defined the role of the new force in these enduring words: 'The Garda Síochána will succeed not by force of arms or numbers, but on their moral authority as servants of the people.'

The goal of a tranquil Irish society incorporated in this mission statement is descriptive of the high ideals on which the police force was founded. There was also a pragmatic side to it, as an armed force would be unlikely to gain the confidence of a people who in many cases had come to view the armed RIC as enforcers of a foreign power, and later had been terrorised by the paramilitary police that replaced the mass resignations of RIC men in 1920 and 1921.

The agonising political divide that existed between the former RIC and IRA men came to a head as William signed on to the new police force. Within the month of May 1922, five RIC men were promoted – one to the rank of deputy commissioner – probably because of their superior knowledge of police work, but some recruits refused to accept these officers (in what became known as the Kildare Mutiny, which lasted from April to August). ·

Despite the troubled climate of the training programme, William Geary and his comrades were hastily 'whipped' into shape to take over policing duties. On 17 August a party of 400 recruits, including William, went by train from Kildare to Kingsbridge Station; they 'fell in', marched to Dublin Castle and, under the command of Commissioner Michael Staines, marched through the gates to take control of the seat of British authority in Ireland. The British flag was lowered, the Irish flag hauled up. Normal duties were performed without arms, but sentries were armed with rifles, and the crack of rifle fire could be heard in the city, where the Civil War was in progress.

Staines tendered his resignation as commissioner on the day following the march into Dublin Castle, due mainly to his disappointment over the Kildare Mutiny and also to the burden of his duties as a member of the Dáil in the formation of the state and his duties in Dublin Corporation. His resignation was accepted with regret on 22 August and he continued to administer the force until 9 September 1922.

General Eoin O'Duffy was then appointed commissioner and held the post until he was removed from office in February 1933. Having sat on the Civic Guard founding committee in the Gresham Hotel, Dublin, with Michael Collins and Staines, he seemed ideally suited to lead the new police force. As commissioner, he founded Coiste Siamsa to promote sport and physical fitness, and was instrumental in establishing the Scott Medal for bravery. He led a large contingent of gardaí on a pilgrimage to Rome in 1928, and in 1932 he was chief marshal at the 31st Eucharistic Congress in Dublin.

William proved to be very proficient in his training, and his past experience as an officer on board ship proved that he had the capacity to take charge, so he was quickly selected for leadership. In September 1922, a mere five months after his induction, he attended a large assembly in a room full of the new police force.

They were addressed by a superintendent and shortly afterwards he was given a uniform and was made acting inspector.

On 26 September Inspector Geary was sent to Clones, County Monaghan, with twenty-two men and a sergeant, to take over the vacant RIC barracks. On 29 September, he went with six men to Ballybay, County Monaghan, where they lived in makeshift billets (if the area had previously had a police station it would probably have been raided and destroyed): the new police units were told to establish control in their selected area. The men had to work in isolation without a dependable chain of command, and without a telephone, lockers, stationery or furniture. It was not uncommon for a man to go to sleep in a bed vacated by another. This was William's first test of leadership; he proved his sterling qualities by maintaining discipline, patrolling the area, keeping the peace and gaining the respect and confidence of the public. The Civic Guards in their smart attire, disciplined and active, were the visible sign of the Irish Free State so essential in a 'border' area where comparison with the RIC was normal.

William subsequently passed the Civil Service Commission 'P' Exam in Irish, English, Mathematics, Geography and efficiency in reportage, which could lead to further promotion.[3] His first serious investigation was a case of infanticide in Ballybay. William related how a young Protestant girl had a baby and abandoned the child. He borrowed a law book from the local coroner and spent all night studying. The next day at the inquest he called the local doctor as a witness and the young girl was returned for trial, which took place in Dublin in the

Central Criminal Court before a sympathetic judge. The girl was released on her own recognisance.

On 9 February 1923 William went on transfer to Carrickmacross, where he was given more responsibilities as a district officer. On 10 October 1923 he was transferred to Monaghan Town, where he would remain for a year. He was promoted to the rank of superintendent on 1 October 1924 and told to purchase a motor car – which shows his superiors' increasing confidence in his work as his area of command was being extended. On 13 October 1924 he was transferred to depot headquarters in Phoenix Park. At headquarters he had complete charge of all activities when, in turn, he was officer of the day. Achieving, as he did, the rank of superintendent with only two years of active service implied that a police career and advancement to higher command could be anticipated.

Soon – on 8 December – Superintendent Geary was transferred to Newport, County Tipperary, and on 4 February 1925 was sent to Templemore. This frequency of transfers was sometimes because of promotion to higher rank and sometimes due to the fact that his ability was needed to solve crime, regain public confidence or improve discipline in the ranks. Even though the Civil War had officially ended in 1923, political subversion on the part of the IRA persisted, and during William's tenure in Templemore a bank robbery was carried out by anti-Treaty forces in Roscrea. Four armed men took £10,617 10s 1d and escaped in a car. The investigation was successful and a conviction secured in the High Court. William Geary recorded:

Thanks to my Sergeant in Templemore, Sgt John Gallagher, we had one man convicted … Ever since then the IRA had a finger on me. Sgt Gallagher kept a diary where he recorded that a man said, 'I'll cut off my ear if I don't have Gallagher fired and Geary reduced.' I was a marked man.[4]

Sergeant Gallagher's secret diary was full of startling revelations about this era in Ireland's history as he cultivated a loyal and dedicated body of informants who spied on criminals and subversives. His full report about the investigation of the Roscrea bank robbery reveals impressive detective work as well as the dark side of intrigue and divided loyalties in those dangerous times.

William was again transferred as superintendent to district headquarters in Kilrush on 10 February 1926. The sub-districts were: Carrigaholt, Doonbeg, Kilrush, Kilkee, Kildysart, Kilmihill, Knock and Labasheeda. The district extended south and west of a line extending through Annaghgeeragh, Doo Lough and Knockalough, and on to Ballycorick Bridge and all the Loop Head coast of more than 100 miles. The area encompassed at least 250 square miles, had eleven significant islands and was served by the famous '3 ft' narrow gauge West Clare Railway, with nine stations and twenty-four level crossings. Superintendent Geary had only fifty-five men to cover this extensive territory.

County Clare was in turmoil due to the activities of the IRA, which persisted with bank robberies, executions, murder, organisation, fundraising, etc. Bands of armed men prevented the unarmed gardaí from carrying out normal duties all over the country. Between 14 November 1922 and 14 November 1926 six gardaí were killed in the Free State.

The head of the anti-Treaty IRA in Kilrush was T. J. Ryan. According to cabinet minutes:

> Consideration was given to a memorandum by the Minister of Home Affairs drawing attention to the continued lawless conditions existing in certain districts namely Leitrim, Mayo, Kerry, Cork, Tipperary and Clare. He had reluctantly come to the conclusion that the only means of dealing with the situation was to ask for an increase of 1,000 men in the Garda Síochána who should be armed and distributed throughout the disturbed areas for the special purpose of dealing with armed crime.[5]

Danger lurked round every corner in this 'most incorrigibly Republican county in the State'.[6] Six weeks before William took charge of Kilrush district headquarters Garda Thomas Dowling had been shot dead at Craggagh, Fanore, County Clare, on 28 December 1925.[7] Many considered Clare to be the most lawless region in the country. Why would the garda commissioner put Superintendent Geary in command of what was tantamount to a war zone?[8] Chief Superintendent Neligan reported, 'I believe he was regarded as fairly efficient', but, as head of intelligence, Neligan must have been well aware of William's success in solving crimes and countering subversion.[9]

On 3 April 1926, seven weeks after William's arrival in Kilrush, the newspaper *Saturday Record* had 'Shooting outrage!'

as its headline. The story below it gave details: 'Motorists ambushed at Tullycrine, near Kilrush, late on Monday night. Joseph Daly, an ex-captain of the National Army residing at Kilmurray, and Michael Gorman were seriously wounded.' In May 1926, when William was on night duty and his car was unattended, the tyres were slashed. He had casts made of the boot prints in the soft earth adjacent to the crime scene; these corresponded with the boots worn by two local youths, but the court said this evidence was not compelling. In another incident, in November 1926, two armed and masked men raided the house of Reverend S. S. King to steal 'poppies' – which they referred to as imperialist propaganda.[10]

The gardaí had to be alert at all times for gunmen: a shot was fired at a garda in Labasheeda in January 1927; twenty volleys of rifle fire were directed at Doonbeg station on 16 April 1927, and one bullet lodged in the headboard of the bed in which Garda Mulligan lay sleeping; and a shot was fired at gardaí dispersing rioters at Knock at midnight on 24 September 1927.[11]

Lingering Civil War tensions, meagre resources, and memories of former harassment by police tended to alienate the citizenry from the Garda Síochána. To counteract this, it was general garda policy to engage in sport, thus providing local and national heroes. In the first ten years gardaí won national and international titles in athletics and boxing, and All Ireland and provincial titles in hurling, football, handball and athletics; were champions in high jump, pole vault and weight throwing in Ireland and Britain, and were involved in the Amateur Athletic Association. In 1927 the *Garda Review* published a picture, with the caption 'Kilrush Garda tug-of-war team', which features the cup won at Kilrush sports with Superintendent Geary in centre.

The *Garda Review* magazine also recorded another policing success in Clare in 1927:

> It is very seldom that the sphinx-like District Justice Gleeson unbends to commend any member of the Garda and when he does one can realise that his commendation is deserved. Recently Superintendent Geary and Detective Officer Coakley came under his favourable comment and still more recently Detective Officer Purcell was highly commended for his ability and perseverance in a difficult and complicated case.[12]

William succeeded in gaining the confidence and cooperation of the population. He was clean living, resourceful, disciplined, dependable, pious and a thorough gentleman. He believed people gained confidence in the garda as things became quiet, and the IRA was frustrated because they were so successful; there was respect for the guards as they did their duty without favour or affectation and they were unarmed. There were problems with hay-burning several times a week, but in one case Sergeant O'Malley collected circumstantial evidence against the culprit. When he was convicted the hay-burning stopped. These burnings were organised by dissident elements to both lessen confidence in the guards and to secure compensation for malicious injury to property.

That the IRA contemplated William's assassination is evident by a curious incident which happened one day in early 1928 when he was in Kilrush. His landlady sent word to him in the barracks that there was a visitor to see him. He walked down from the barracks and met a beautiful young lady, handsomely dressed, whom he did not know. He thought she might have some information for him and asked his landlady to give them some tea in the dining-room. They spoke for about twenty minutes and then the young lady decided to leave. William never saw her again. He later found out that there were rumours that the IRA had plans to shoot him and that the girl had been sent as a decoy to make a date and bring him out to the countryside. But she had not tried to seduce him, and had never even smiled. She had probably realised that he would be shot if he went to meet with her. His dismissal from the Garda Síochána probably saved his life, as he left Kilrush.[13]

By June of 1928 life was good for Superintendent Geary. His police administration was successful, his men were loyal and diligent, and comparative peace existed in the community. William was at the peak of his professional career. At his last court appearance as prosecutor in Kilrush, on 6 June 1928, his success in creating a peaceful civic situation is reflected in the mundane list of cases to be heard:

1   Rowdy visitor in the County Home.

2   Donkey and cart left unattended.

3   Playing handball on the street.

4   Failing to send children to school.

5   Application by Lizzie O'Brien to have Annie Downes bound to the peace.

6   Application for a general exemption order for the public
     houses on the occasion of the Kerry vs. Clare Championship.[14]

5

An Accusation

In June 1928 Deputy Commissioner Éamonn Coogan was on an inspection tour of County Clare and was expected in Kilrush on 16 June. William thought nothing could go wrong, but on the day he received a message to meet Chief Superintendent Edward O'Duffy, his local superior in County Clare, and was told to be in Ennis, in uniform, at 10 a.m.[1] Garda John McLynn drove William from Kilrush to Ennis; William thought he might be complimented because of the improved conditions in West Clare.

He walked over to Carmody's Hotel with Chief Superintendent O'Duffy and the first time he had any inkling of trouble was when Chief Superintendent O'Duffy said, 'Your life is ruined. You'd better tell the truth.'[2] Commissioner Eoin O'Duffy, Deputy Commissioner Coogan and Chief Superintendent David Neligan sat at one side of the table in the room. They were men with power, unaccustomed to being questioned or opposed. Two of them had risked their lives in the fight for Irish freedom; Neligan, working as he did in shadowy intelligence operations for the British administration in Dublin

Castle, repeatedly risked a fate 'worse than death'. However, the unfettered power they now had, their unencumbered egos and the pressures of the political situation combined to make them careless of Superintendent Geary's legal rights.

Coogan was a native of Kilkenny. He had joined the Irish Volunteers in 1914 and was later an IRA and Sinn Féin organiser; in the 12th Dáil he was Fine Gael TD for Kilkenny. He was well educated – a graduate of Trinity College, Dublin, with Bachelor of Science, Bachelor of Commerce and Bachelor of Law degrees. He studied Greek, was a gold-medal Latin scholar, and spoke French fluently. At various times he was vice principal of the Technical Institute, Athlone, principal of the Limerick School of Commerce and vice president of the Technical Institute of Limerick. He married Beatrice Toal, a policeman's daughter. Coogan was an inspector in the Department of Local Government when he was invited to join the Garda Síochána by the Taoiseach William T. Cosgrave. He was given the rank of assistant commissioner in September 1922, and in January 1923 was promoted to deputy commissioner.[3] Coogan had a caring disposition and strove to uphold the honour of the Garda Síochána. When the Garda Síochána Medical Aid Society was founded in June 1934, Coogan was among the first trustees.

Coogan's sense of justice, fair play and courage was seen in his backing of Maurice Riordan. In March 1923 IRA prisoners of the Free State Army were killed at Bahagh, Caherciveen, in County Kerry. Although exonerated by a military tribunal, Lieutenants Harrington and McCarthy of the Free State Army resigned their commissions as they knew Free State troops had made and detonated the explosives used in the unlawful killings. After the deaths, Maurice Riordan subsequently made a claim for the loss of his son. A letter from Coogan accompanied his claim, dated 23 December 1923, saying: 'The facts were true; that William Riordan was an "irregular" and was one of a captured column with arms; temporarily imprisoned in the "workhouse", Caherciveen. He was taken from there and done to death with four other prisoners.'[4]

At William's interrogation in Carmody's Hotel, Eoin O'Duffy presided; any decision or procedure would have to have his approval. Neligan, who had been instrumental in founding the Special Branch, was at that time acting as head of intelligence.[5] Coogan does not appear to have taken a significant part in the proceedings, but it cannot be said that he did his sworn duty to enforce the law without 'fear or favour, malice or ill will'. The ardour he had for justice and law enforcement in 1923 seems to have diminished by 1928 and, given his position in the garda, he could hardly have claimed ignorance of the law.

The meeting was curt and devoid of formalities; confronted by O'Duffy, Coogan and Neligan, William said he saluted and the commissioner said, 'Sit down.' He told him, 'We have evidence that you took a bribe of £100 for information that you gave to the republicans, I have your signature in receipt of money and can you explain that.'[6] William was shocked, and told the commissioner it must be a plot. Then Neligan stood up and searched him.

The crude nature of the confrontation was designed to take

William by surprise. Commissioner O'Duffy included the following in the report he wrote four days later about it:

> It was considered that the element of surprise should be worked to full advantage, and that he should not get time to consider his line of defence, and being regarded as a bit weak willed there was the possibility that he might break down and admit at least some of his dealings with the enemies of the State.[7]

William gave a spirited response. O'Duffy's report stated that he was:

> … quite normal and proclaimed his innocence. He asserted that he was not at any time in touch with the Irregulars, directly or indirectly, that he never received any money from them, that they were his enemies, that he carried out his duties towards them fearlessly, that this was a diabolical plot on the part of Ryan and Co. [the IRA] to injure him, that although he might be punished now, time would vindicate him, and that all concerned would be forced to apologise to him for the terrible accusations made.[8]

O'Duffy did not have an incriminating signature – what he had was a decoded IRA message that named 'supt geary' as the recipient of £100. The decrypted IRA message read:

> have handed over the hundrep [*sic*] pounds to supt geary he was very satisfied with the amount i have given him list of houses which can be safely raided from time to time it would be well to hit up geary

as hard as possible in an phoblacht as he is working satisfactory let
me know if i may drop the other cid haue [*sic*] sent on by courier
the latest stuff as it is important you should have it at once.[9]

Coogan asked a couple of questions merely to check the veracity
of Superintendent Geary's reported conversation with Detective
Officer Keyes in Kilrush, while he was overseeing operations
against the IRA (see Appendix 2).

O'Duffy lived for sixteen years after this encounter, long
enough to learn that William was not weak-willed, but rather
was sufficiently resolute to carry on the quest for years to have
his honour restored.

Both the element of surprise in William's interrogation and
O'Duffy's bluster, 'I have your signature', had failed completely.
Neligan, with the assistance of two Dublin detectives, searched
everything belonging to William, including his accommodation,
as well as properties of IRA suspects, but they found nothing
incriminating. O'Duffy was faced with a dilemma – he had no
reason for an arrest, so he decided that Superintendent Geary
was to be suspended from duty and told him to report to the
depot headquarters in Dublin to await the outcome of the
investigation.

William arrived at the garda depot on 18 June 1928. As
the investigation was *sub judice* he was generally avoided, but
was visited by his friend Superintendent Mick Higgins, who
was stationed in Thurles, County Tipperary; he had previously
collaborated with William to arrest the Roscrea bank robbers.
Higgins told him of a conversation he had had with Neligan to

the effect that he was to be 'booted out of the force'. The next day William Geary wrote a lucid statement of the circumstances (later referred to by O'Duffy as 'document E') to the adjutant, Commandant Stack, under the heading: 'Re engaging of a Solicitor – Supt. W Geary. R.O. C.241, August 1927'. In the second paragraph he wrote:

> My integrity, character, honour and family has been besmirched by the action of my authorities on 16th June 1928, so it is up to me now to protect myself, and to do so I request authority to employ a Solicitor with necessary assistance, who will go into this matter with me. In the circumstances I do not think that my request is unreasonable.[10]

William quoted a Routine Order that expressed his civil right to legal counsel. It is evident that the adjutant urgently contacted the commissioner and a state of alarm ensued, because the malpractice, secrecy and failure to concede natural justice of those accusing William would have been exposed. William received no response to his request.[11]

Later he described the conditions of his stay at garda headquarters:

> In the Depot I slept and had meals in the Officers Quarters. I had one visitor – Superintendent Higgins, with whom I was friendly and served with me in County Tipperary. Why he was in Dublin I did not know … All the time I was in the Depot I expected a Court of Inquiry to start. There was none.[12]

The fact that there was to be no investigation rested in part on the lack of evidence and on the character of O'Duffy, the decision-maker, as he would not take advice from anyone and arrogantly trusted his initial judgement without investigating the situation further.

Neligan submitted a report titled 'Irregular Papers Implicating Superintendent Geary' to O'Duffy.[13] (The term 'Irregular' referred to the anti-Treaty IRA.) The next course of action, to verify the treachery, should have been to direct unique information not divulged to anyone else to Superintendent Geary, with a view to procuring compelling evidence, and then to see what reaction this would evoke from the IRA. Additionally the IRA letter should have been tested for fingerprints and submitted to a handwriting expert to compare with the writing of known suspects. However, Neligan's report records only a series of twenty-seven questions and answers posed and answered by himself (see Appendix 2 for full text). For example:

Question 3. Were they aware that this code could be deciphered by us?

Answer. No. They had recently changed over to a new and far more difficult code, and it was given out in Court lately that the police could not decode 'I.R.A.' messages.

On page one of this report Neligan says, 'There are a great number of such code messages on our files.' Presumably, as head of security, he had some expertise in this area; therefore his answer to the question quoted above is at variance with the known fact that the code had been in use for at least two years.[14]

Another example from Neligan's report reads:

Question 4. What are Geary's previous political history and connections?

Answer. It would appear that he never participated in the Volunteer movement …

It is incomprehensible that the garda head of security, who had spent two weeks preparing for the confrontation, had failed to examine Superintendent Geary's personal file, where it was recorded that the Officer Commanding of 'F' Coy, 3 Battalion, West Limerick Brigade, Seán Ó Brosnacháin, had certified that William Geary had 'discharged all his duties in a manner worthy of an exemplary soldier'.

A further example from Neligan's report reads:

Question 8. His ability as an Officer?

Answer. I believe he is regarded as fairly efficient, although he did not distinguish himself in the Roscrea bank robbery case.

This assertion is diametrically opposed to the facts of which Neligan and O'Duffy were fully aware. The Roscrea bank robbery occurred at 3 p.m. on 24 March 1925; Neligan visited

Superintendent Geary's District Headquarters the following day. By 29 March the names of the robbers eventually arrested and charged – James Peters, John McCarthy and Michael O'Brien, all from Thurles, County Tipperary – were known through good investigative methods. Sergeant John Gallagher and Detective Devoy met O'Duffy and Neligan in Dublin on 1 April 1925, and on 10 April Peters, McCarthy and O'Brien were arrested and charged. O'Duffy was present at the identification parade. The trial in the Central Criminal Court in early November convicted Michael O'Brien despite the wholesale intimidation of witnesses and the non-cooperation of the bank officials, two of whom were considered suspect and dismissed shortly afterwards on a small pension. The informers, the investigators and the witnesses were all in mortal danger during the investigation, trial and aftermath; there was cogent evidence of all this in handwritten reports and in the newspaper columns.

Neligan's report of questions and answers is characterised by speculation, unsupported inferences and untruths, later admitted by Neligan in his correspondence with William. The report contains no compelling evidence and the closing paragraphs are revealing:

Starting out with the firm conviction that the Supt. is guilty of this grave charge, it would be unnatural if bias against him did not creep in to fashion my thoughts and words but, I have as far as possible tried to fairly set out the facts of the case and draw reasonable deductions and inferences therefrom. The evidence against him is incomplete no doubt, as it must be in such cases, but it is sufficient in my opinion to be incontrovertible.

I have to strongly recommend that this man, whom I believe to have betrayed his trust and besmirched the good name of the force, be dismissed with ignominy.

It defies logic that a senior police officer such as Neligan, head of security, would be party to a contrivance like this; he apparently conspired in the certain knowledge that Commissioner O'Duffy would approve.

O'Duffy, armed with the report of the head of the garda intelligence department, and in an effort to get rid of William Geary before he might open up a 'can of worms', hastily prepared his own report for the secretary of the Department of Justice:

20 June 1928

The Secretary,
Department of Justice

Alleged Treachery – Supt. Geary, Kilrush

The attached report from Chief Superintendent Neligan re above is very comprehensive and does not require much elaboration from me. It has been prepared after several discussions during the past fortnight.

The receipt of the copy of letter from the Irregular D/I to the O/C West Clare was one of the greatest shocks I ever got.

It was almost incredible that in the ranks of the Garda Síochána a creature could be found so base and so treacherous. I could understand information leaking out to the Irregulars owing to loose talk on the part of the members of the lower ranks, though such is unlikely and has not come under notice. I could also understand members, through a false idea of patriotism, or in order to court popularity with a certain section, or through sheer cowardice, deliberately giving information. Such conduct in a Police Force would be reprehensible, and would be punished by prompt dismissal, but a person who would descend so low as to sell the secrets entrusted to him as an Officer of the Police Force of the State, is a criminal of the vilest type and richly deserves capital punishment. (The question of including such a provision in future legislation is worthy of serious consideration).

I was entrusted by the late General Collins with meeting the various members of the RIC in Ulster who were assisting the Volunteers, and later I met the helpful members from the rest of Ireland, and I can safely assert that in not a single instance did they seek money. I believe had they been offered money they would be very much insulted.

We had many anxious moments, while waiting to get the cipher message decoded, going through the various Officers, NCOs and Gardaí in Co. Clare, and strangely enough I had strong suspicion of Superintendent Geary. At a recent Conference of the Superintendents of Limerick, Clare and Tipperary, held in Limerick, Superintendent Geary stood out alone on his remarkable knowledge of the Irregular Organisation in his area, and was particularly outspoken when referring to the blackguardism of Ryan and his principal followers in Clare. At these conferences I dealt at great length with the Irregular Organisation and stressed the necessity for close surveillance, frequent holds up, and searches, etc., differentiating between those who adopted constitutional methods as against those whose policy is to overthrow the State by violence. I referred to the latter as criminals, visualised their possible activities – assassination, raids on Garda Stations, and robbery of Banks (I was aware at the time that Ryan was making arrangements to rob a Bank in Ennis) and pointed out that their efforts must be frustrated, that one successful Bank robbery was more serious, and had a more adverse effect on the prestige of the State than any epidemic of ordinary crime. I further dwelt on members of the Force playing a safe game, courting popularity with criminals, etc. I am of opinion that this is 'the latest stuff' referred to in document 'B' attached.

Immediately we received the decoded messages I got in touch with the Department and explained the position verbally to the Minister. Apart altogether from the question of dismissal, I urged the necessity for criminal action, as I feel that anything in the nature of treachery in the Garda must be dealt with in a most drastic fashion. It was considered, however, that we could not make use of the evidence we had in the open Court, that it would be improper to make public the manner in which we secured copies and photographs of the correspondence, and further, that we could not very well publish the manner in which we got the code message deciphered. It was decided that I, accompanied by Chief Superintendent Neligan, should proceed immediately to Co. Clare with the hope of getting additional evidence. There was a possibility that a search of Superintendent Geary's person, his office and house, might reveal something. It was further decided that the houses of Ryan and other prominent Irregulars should be searched simultaneously with the search of Superintendent Geary's house.

We arrived in Limerick at 10 p.m. on the same evening, and a Conference was held at which were present, Commissioner, Deputy Commissioner Coogan (who is presently on inspection in Clare), Chief Superintendents Neligan, O'Duffy and Burke. It was decided that Chief Superintendent O'Duffy should instruct Superintendent Geary to report to him in Ennis at 10 a.m. the following morning. Superintendent Geary was paraded before the Commissioner, D.C. Coogan, Chief Superintendent Neligan and Chief Superintendent O'Duffy, and I immediately charged him with treachery, informing him I had definite and indisputable proof of his acts. It was considered that the element of surprise should be worked to full advantage, that he should not get time to consider his line of defence, and being regarded as a bit weak willed, there was the possibility that he might break down and admit at least some of his dealings with the enemies of the State. We had no doubts in our minds as to his own guilt, but we had hopes that he might give us the name of the 'high official' in Cork with whom he, Geary, put the Irregulars in touch. (See document 'A' attached). I considered the securing of this information of premier importance as one 'wrong' Officer should undermine the whole Organisation of the Garda as far as dealing with political crime is concerned.

When confronted by his Commissioner with the most

serious charge that could be made against a Police Officer, the Superintendent did not show by his appearance, or actions, any surprise. He blushed somewhat at first, but was quite normal and proclaimed his innocence. He asserted that he was not at any time in touch with the Irregulars directly or indirectly, that he never received any money from them, that they were his enemies, that he carried out his duties towards them fearlessly, that this was a diabolical plot on the part of Ryan and Co. to injure him, that although he might be punished now, time would vindicate him, and that all concerned would be forced to apologise to him for the terrible accusations made. In view of this attitude there was nothing to be gained by pursuing the interrogations further.

I then informed him that he must submit to a search of his person. He at once turned out his pockets, his boots and stockings, and portion of his uniform were taken off, but the examination revealed nothing incriminating so far as the charge was concerned, except that he had in his note book the name and address of Michael Comyn. When asked who was this Michael Comyn he said 'that is a gentleman interested in mining in West Clare'. On looking up a Directory, however, we found that the address was that of Michael Comyn, KC. He expressed surprise at this. It is but just to add here that the greater portion of his personal correspondence was with the most reliable Officers and Sergeants of the Garda Síochána.

His office and rooms at Kilrush were later very thoroughly searched, bank books and personal belongings examined, but nothing was found. Simultaneously the houses of Ryan and other Irregulars were searched with like result.

Before leaving the District I suspended the Superintendent from duty, and directed him to report to the Depot on the 18th instant. Two service revolvers and ammunition found in his possession were taken from him.

After he received the notice of suspension he said to Superintendent Kelleher, 'Some member of the Force has been giving away information, they suspected me, and I am now suspended. I leave the Force with a clean conscience'. He also intimated that he would dispose of his car immediately.

When he returned to Kilrush after being suspended he sent for his clerk, Guard Corbett, and enquired from him what questions were put to him (Garda Corbett was also interrogated previously). The Garda not knowing the Superintendent was suspended gave him a full account of the questions and answers. The Superintendent then informed the clerk that he (the Superintendent) was suspended and added 'Ryan and the others will have a laugh now'.

Superintendent Geary arrived in the Depot on the evening of the 18th instant, and on the 19th I received communication marked 'E' from him. On being warned by the Adjutant that the minute was intemperate, if not insubordinate, Superintendent Geary stated he wished it to be sent along to the Commissioner in its present form.

I attach a supplementary report marked 'F' from Chief Superintendent Neligan, referring to an incident with a gentleman named Connihan of Kilrush. When I asked Geary what was Connihan's politics he answered 'Imperialist'.

I think I have now given a full history of the case, and it only remains for me to make my recommendation.

After giving the matter very full consideration from every point of view, and after discussing the matter with the members of Headquarters Staff, I have come to the conclusion that the Superintendent is guilty of treachery, and I recommend that he be dismissed from the Force with ignominy forthwith. No useful purpose would be served by framing charges and holding an Enquiry, and I accordingly request the dismissal of this Officer in accordance with the terms of Section 24 and 25 of the Discipline Regulations, 1926.

In view of the request in the Superintendent's letter of 19th instant (document 'E') to which I have not replied, and owing to the nature of the case, it is very desirable that the matter be dealt with immediately.

[The photocopy of the original shows the signature of Eoin O'Duffy]
COMMISSIONER[15]

The report offered no evidence to support a criminal charge against William Geary. Neligan should have investigated and reported to the commissioner, who in turn would then appraise the evidence and, if warranted, initiate disciplinary action or a criminal prosecution. If this was upheld the commissioner would then report to the secretary of the Department of Justice seeking a dismissal. What happened was a travesty of justice.

The commissioner failed to comply with section 7 of the Garda Síochána (Discipline) Regulations 1926 when the serious allegations were denied by Superintendent Geary and should have given the accused a written account of the charges on a Misconduct Form. Not only did he fail to comply with statute law, but he also denied William the rights conferred on him by the Routine Orders of the Garda Síochána (R.O. 241 of August 1927), which he had issued ten months previously.[16] Section 8 of Routine Orders required that 'the Commissioner shall direct a sworn enquiry to be held to inquire and examine on oath into the truth of the charge preferred'.

A further example of O'Duffy's lack of scruple in defaming anyone he deemed expendable is his letter to the Department of Justice on 9 November 1928 concerning the dismissal of a detective officer, John Coakley.[17] O'Duffy wrote: 'During the greater portion of the time he served under ex-Superintendent Geary, who was dismissed the Force in June of this year for treachery. The bad influence of a treacherous officer was bound to have an effect on the outlook of Coakley.'[18] Actually Coakley had served under District Officer Geary for only approximately nineteen per cent of his service in the sub-districts of Knock, as acting sergeant, and at Kilrush.[19]

Sergeant John Gallagher of Templemore was a very accomplished investigator, whose secret diary has already been mentioned. He had a team of six spies – always referred to by numbers, never by name in his reports – and they provided invaluable information about the IRA. In a very revealing entry written a mere five weeks after William's dismissal, Gallagher recorded the following information, provided by an informer:

He also told me that there was something mysterious about Sup't

At Cloonee Cottage, Ballyagran, *c.* 1905, (*l to r*) Patrick Geary, Mrs Patrick Geary, baby Julia Geary, Thomas Geary (in petticoat), William Geary, Mary Ellen Keane. *Courtesy of Geary archives, the Garda Museum.*

On 17 August 1922 Commissioner Michael Staines, with 400 gardaí, marched in to take over Dublin Castle. *Courtesy of the Garda Museum, Dublin Castle.*

Superintendent William Geary (with trophy) and his victorious Garda tug-of-war team, Kilrush 1926. *Courtesy of Garda Review.*

Inspector William Geary, Reg. No. 938, at Carrickmacross in July 1923. *Private Collection.*

Sergeant John Gallagher, Reg. No. 2225, a friend and colleague of William Geary. *Private Collection.*

Deputy Commissioner Éamonn Coogan, (1896–1948) B.Sc., B.Comm., B.L.: he represented Kilkenny as a Fine Gael Deputy. *Courtesy of Garda Museum, Dublin Castle.*

Garda Commissioner Eoin O'Duffy (1892–1944): he saw active service in Cogadh na Saoirse, was made Europe's youngest General in 1922, and was a founder member of An Garda Síochána. *Courtesy of Jim Herlihy, FGSI.*

I, Intelligence
H.Q.   West Clare Bn
                                                        5 - 6 - 28

acknowledge receipt of yours of the
inst Ref No U N O 112 which reached
safely on the 4th. I have noted instructions
tained therein.

Attached herewith receipt for £100-0-0
received from G. H. Q. Officer for Special
Intelligence.

(3) £12 HRVRT EIHNE IERSB OCWES EVRDE
OAAHG FADTW ASOWA OHEIT OLEVP ESTEO
CIOEE OHSFN TVRSP UCNNS SDTHW ETOIR
IASEY CBATO TOPGY HVTHA TBGPP ISKPA
UTMON ATNYI AVOBD MLYSL RTIOE RFTHH
HTWIU HEAOT OHLHN YMEOE STEER PEIHI
IYMLU AAHTM RDCES STAUO AENIS FMWHA
ETGLA RNLIY IVHDH SMEUE FELAI AKOFT●
NTFAA DETRT ASCRE DPSNE IEOHO SIHOE
ESEFO NSSRI TSBCI RIHTH ANVDD UVWIL
HLIUT DNSAT DIY.TI UA.

(4) Relating the agents in Limerick it is rather
difficult for me to size up their mentality
I should think they would be satisfied
with something around £50-0-0. Am pleased
that the official in Cork is all right.

                        O. C. West Clare Bn.

IRA coded letter dated 5 June 1928 devised by the IRA in Kilrush to
incriminate Superintendent William Geary. *Courtesy of the Department
of Justice, Equality and Law Reform records.*

B

Have handed over the hundred pounds to Superintendent Geary. He was very satisfied with the amount. I have given him list of houses which can be safely raided from time to time. It would be well to hit up Geary as hard as possible in AN PHOELACHT (?) (sic) as he is working satisfactory. (Let me know if I may drop the other C.I.D.) Have sent on by courier the latest stuff as it is important you should have it at once.

Document 'B' to support Commissioner O'Duffy's request for William Geary's dismissal; decoded by Colonel Carter, Scotland Yard. *Courtesy of the Garda Museum, Dublin Castle.*

Chief Super-intendent David Neligan: Colonel in the Free State Army, head of Garda Security and founder of Special Branch Detectives. *Courtesy of the Garda Museum, Dublin Castle.*

Sergeant William Geary, 1243938, in the uniform of the USA Air Transport Finance Command. *Courtesy of the Garda Museum, Dublin Castle.*

The Honourable John Patrick Collins, Judge of the Supreme Court of the State of New York, godson of the late William Geary, KHS. *Private collection.*

Superintendent Tim Leahy, who procured publicity that brought success to William Geary's quest. *Private collection.*

Mr John O'Donoghue, TD, Irish Minister for Justice, with William Geary in Manhattan, New York in November 1999. *Courtesy of Higgins/ Reuters and The Irish Times.*

William Geary with his regalia after investiture as Knight in the Equestrian Order of the Holy Sepulchre of Jerusalem, 15 September 2000. *Courtesy of The Irish Times/Geary family collection.*

William Geary, KHS, at the age of 104. *Courtesy of Irish Voice, New York.*

Mr Bertie Ahern, TD, former Taoiseach. *Courtesy of Constituency Office, Drumcondra, Dublin.*

Mr John O'Donoghue, TD, former Minister for Justice. *Courtesy of Constituency Office, Tralee, Co. Kerry.*

Margaret Ward, *Irish Times* journalist who revealed William Geary's story. *Private collection.*

Conor Brady, former editor of *The Irish Times*. *Private collection.*

Geary being dismissed, that he was speaking to a prominent Republican who said he knew that the receipt found, on which he was dismissed, was a forgery and that it was done intentionally by the Republicans on account of all the harm he did them in Clare since he went there.

He asked me if I would be interested in a big arms dump in Kildare and that he would be in a position to help me. I said I would but that owing to the regulations of our new Chief Supt I would have to tell my Supt when and where I was going and the business I was going on, he replied that as Tipp' men were mixed up in the case and the Supt was a Tipp' man he would not agree so it was decided to drop it.[20]

The first paragraph is significant because although Superintendent Geary's dismissal was reported in the papers, the non-existent receipt was not mentioned. How could the republicans have known about this pseudo receipt?

The second paragraph from Gallagher's diary reveals the nature of counter-espionage at the time, and the lack of trust in some members of the police who had been comrades-in-arms with former IRA members. It also shows the continuing threat to state security long after the Civil War.

The hearing in Ennis on 16 June 1928 set in motion a sequence of events which culminated in the dismissal of William Geary on 25 June by an order of the Executive Council and signed by the president, William T. Cosgrave.[21] For William Geary this was the nadir of his career and his whole life; his good reputation and family honour were destroyed. Commissioner O'Duffy and

Chief Superintendent Neligan ineptly became pawns in the conspiracy of the IRA.

A case can be made that the alliance of O'Duffy and Neligan was not merely a dereliction of duty but an active involvement in tyrannical conduct specifically forbidden by the regulations. These senior officers could have been charged with breaches of the discipline regulations, although given the lawless climate of the times this was unlikely.[22] President Cosgrave also bears some responsibility in the miscarriage of justice: while a president had to delegate responsibility to persons such as Commissioner O'Duffy and the Minister of Justice, James Fitzgerald Kenney, it seems clear from the reports that William Geary was being denied due process. Whatever the individual factors of incompetence, lawlessness or vindictiveness, the system of governance facilitated the IRA.

6

STRIVING FOR VINDICATION

William Geary was a sociable and upright man. He had enjoyed six years of Garda Síochána service, although every day was fraught with danger due to the Civil War and later sedition.[1] The life he shared with his comrades created strong bonds; his dismissal wrenched him away from his companions and destroyed his prospects of a great career. The depths of his loneliness and despondency must have been great.

Before leaving Dublin, after his dismissal, William called on Chief Superintendent Neligan in his office. Neligan told him that if he cooperated with the investigation and provided information about his presumed contacts in the IRA he would receive a job with the government. But William did not want to play that game! He said he could not add anything to what he had already said because he was not involved in bribery; he told Neligan that he was not guilty. He returned to Kilrush, paid his bills, sold his car, went home to Ballyagran and found solace in life on the farm. Because he was damned as a traitor, there were no opportunities for him in Ireland. He could not work as a solicitor, or in the bank; he had to emigrate.

He left for the United States in November 1928, on the SS *Baltic* and arrived in New York on 5 December 1928.[2] He had intended to go to Chicago, but on the voyage he met Gerald McInerney, who prevailed on him to stay in New York, where he boarded with Gerald's aunt. Conscious of his need for further education if he was to succeed in life, William immediately began his high-school education. In January 1929 he started night classes at George Washington High School in Manhattan.

He visited Mary Ellen Keane, who had been a family servant at Cloonee Cottage. She was married to Michael Faye. Mary Ellen first secured a job for him in Bloomingdales Department Store at $22 per week, and later found him work at Buckley Newhall Furnishings. Then, with the help of Dr Flynn, the family doctor, in August 1929 William was hired by Consolidated Edison Company Inc. (popularly known as Con Edison), which supplied gas, steam and electricity in New York City. At first he was employed as a labourer, 'digging holes', then in pulling 'laterals' – the service cables from the underground electric utility – to dwellings. Being of slight build and having not engaged in physical labour for a number of years, he did not find this work easy, but he said, 'It was not bad.'[3] His employment with Con Edison advanced to distributing bills and collecting monies from clients and finally to being ledger clerk, taking charge of the books and earning $38 per week.

The work-week at that time included a half-day on Saturday. So in the beginning William had to contend with a five-and-a-half-day work-week and high-school classes at night. With his advancement to bill collector his work hours became less onerous and he continued his evening education until he graduated in Chemistry, Biology, Physics, Algebra and English in June 1933. He also studied French at Columbia University for one semester. These were the years of the Great Depression, with mass unemployment becoming an enormous challenge in 1933, and this may have affected his decision not to pursue higher education further.

In addition to his intense self-improvement programme, he was involved in fraternal and volunteer work. In the course of time, he became secretary of the Limerick Men's Benevolent and Social Association, and then president of that organisation in 1936, 1937 and 1940. He joined the Irish fraternal organisation Clan na nGael and was active in the Catholic charity St Vincent de Paul Society.

In the midst of all this activity, he did not forget that his honour had been besmirched. Bolstered by his growing sense of achievement, in 1934 he made the first of many attempts to clear his name. He worked with his cousin Michael D. Fitzgerald to prepare an affidavit concerning the events of 1928 and sent it to his brother Michael in Rathkeale, County Limerick. Being in New York, William was concerned because he was isolated from those who could advance his cause due to poor communications; he had anticipated ongoing investigation of his case but this never transpired. The prospect was growing hopeless, so he sent his case for scrutiny to the Minister for Justice, P. J. Rutledge, and had Donncada Ó Briain, TD, acting on his behalf.

Despite the absence of evidence against William, Rutledge responded to the appeal of Ó Briain on 16 April 1934 as follows:

I have the papers before me in the case of ex-Superintendent William Geary and I am satisfied that there would need to be some fresh facts, other than a re-affirmation of innocence on the part of Mr Geary himself to justify the reconsideration of a decision which was reached after a full and fair consideration on very clear evidence. Really I do not think that this is a case in which you should interest yourself further.

I am returning the papers which you handed to me the other day.[4]

The minister erred in this decision because Geary was not appealing a criminal or internal administrative conviction; a judicial process did not bring about his dismissal.

It was many years before William began to protest against the injustice again, other than to engage with the Limerick Men's Association and to correspond informally with friends. He had to wait for the political regime to change to one that would not be hostile to his cause.

In the Second World War Geary, being younger than forty-seven, was registered as A1 in the draft. In August 1942 he was sworn in at Governor's Island to serve his adopted country.[5] He had two weeks to put his affairs in order and then was ordered to Long Island, where he was given a series of IQ tests. At 2 a.m. one morning a sergeant came to him, saying something along the lines of, 'You came in here two weeks ago. You get yourself into the air force, and you are going down to Memphis tomorrow in charge of three men …'[6]

However, before he went to Memphis, William was in Nashville, Tennessee, and then in Long Beach, California, to learn the basics of army finance. On graduating from the military school, he was sent to Memphis to serve in the United States Air Force, Air Transport Command Finance. He was promoted to corporal right away; shortly afterwards he was given the rank of sergeant in charge of the payroll at the base. He also paid the airmen who ferried planes to Africa for use in the war effort, after they returned to base. He paid out thousands of dollars every day, but the only time he held a gun was on his way to collect bags of money.

When he was in the air force, he earned $38 a week. Room and board cost him $15, he could buy a suit for $20, cigarettes cost 11 cents, and, after prohibition, a quart of Old Kentucky Whiskey was $2. He thought he had the best job in the forces. Six months into his military service, on 10 February 1943, he married Margaret Shryane from Rooskey, Ballaghaderreen, County Roscommon. After his honourable discharge from the United States forces, the couple lived in Manhattan, and William returned to his job with Consolidated Edison Company Inc.

In 1950, twenty-two years after William's dismissal from the Garda Síochána, his case was the subject of enquiry within the Department of Justice and with the garda commissioner, for reasons that are not entirely clear now. Several handwritten minutes were exchanged on 6, 8 and 12 July 1950. In one of these, the secretary of the Department of Justice wrote an informal note to the garda commissioner as follows:

I am directed by the Minister for Justice to refer to your minute (B.4327/28 of 26 June 1928 [when the file was opened]) regarding the dismissal of Superintendent William Geary from the Garda Síochána and I am to state that he would be glad to learn the reasons for which Mr Geary was dismissed and in particular whether it followed disciplinary charges.[7]

In reply, the last paragraph from the commissioner's office letter stated:

No disciplinary charges were preferred against him and no papers are available here to indicate the reasons for his suspension and dismissal. It was known generally throughout the Force at the time that he was dismissed for disloyalty in passing information, etc., to the IRA.[8]

A handwritten note on the margin of the letter, dated 1 August 1950, says, 'I showed this to the Minister. He agreed that we would take no further action.'[9]

Deputy David Madden, Fine Gael, from the new constituency of West Limerick (William's home), instigated this enquiry. Collectively the people who left William to endure dishonour after the inquiry had been instigated were Taoiseach John A. Costello, who had been the attorney general in the government that dismissed Superintendent Geary in 1928; General Seán Mac Eoin, Minister for Justice, who would have known David Neligan very well, having served in the army with him; the garda commissioner Michael Kinnane, LLB, who was commissioner from 1938 to 1952 and whose knowledge of the law and garda administration was considerable; and Daniel Costigan, assistant secretary of the Department of Justice, who had succeeded Commissioner Michael Kinnane when he died while still in office.

During this time, William was engrossed in the life of his family. He and Margaret had two daughters, Helen and Anne, so there were family events such as baptisms, confirmations, outings and holidays, and family concerns such as anxieties about schooling and financial affairs to contend with. Later, college expenditures, weddings and grandchildren commanded William's attention. He had the good fortune to have stable employment until he retired from Con Edison in 1967, thirty-eight years after he joined the company.

By a strange twist of fate the town of Kilrush and the local IRA chief, T. J. Ryan, author of the documents used to dishonour William, featured in the disgrace of Chief Superintendent David Neligan. Indiscipline in the Special Branch led to unlawful excesses in many parts of the country, which reflected badly on Neligan. On Sunday 14 August 1932, at Kilrush, T. J. Ryan and George Gilmore were shot by 'S' Branch detective officers Myles Muldowney and Michael Christopher Carroll. For this crime they were dismissed, after the Kilrush Enquiry Report on 15 September (see Appendix 4 for the full text of the report). Neligan was furious and, with Commissioner O'Duffy's approval, he organised a collection on behalf of the dismissed detectives, in a circular issued on 8 November 1932 by Sergeant P. J. Gallagher, secretary of the Joint Representative

Bodies for all ranks. The Minister for Justice, James Geoghegan, reprimanded O'Duffy, and Eamon de Valera, influenced by his republican followers, dismissed Neligan and relegated him to an obscure post in the Land Commission.

Others who featured directly, either by action or acquiescence, in the decision to dismiss William Geary passed to their eternal reward: James Fitzgerald Kenney, SC, who was Minister of Justice in 1928 and consented to the O'Duffy report, died in 1932; O'Duffy, whose image went from hero to hopeless, died in 1944; Deputy Commissioner Coogan, whose virtuous defence of IRA prisoners was commendable, but who abandoned William in his hour of need in Kilrush, died in 1948; P. J. Rutledge, Minister for Justice, to whom William Geary addressed his first appeal in 1934, died in 1952; T. J. Ryan of Cranny and Kilrush died in 1962, but he was never likely to reveal IRA secrets and his ardour for the republican cause was as strong as Geary's determination for the rule of law; William T. Cosgrave, president of the Executive Council in 1928, who signed the order of William Geary's dismissal, died in 1965.

A Renewed Effort to Restore His Good Name

In 1968 the recently retired William Geary had a friend plead his case with the Irish prime minister. The Reverend Donald K. O'Callaghan, Order of Carmelites, from the priory of St Simon Stock in the Bronx, New York, wrote on 22 March 1968 to the Taoiseach, Jack Lynch. O'Callaghan, eulogising William, appealed for clemency for him; to achieve this he said William was willing to forgo all claim to compensation and would not take a case against the state for damages.

Lynch acknowledged O'Callaghan's letter six days later, and undertook to pass the request to Michael Moran, the Minister for Justice. In fact, a copy was passed to the minister's private secretary 'for suitable draft reply'. Moran's private secretary in the Department of Justice wrote to the private secretary of the Taoiseach on 10 April 1968; among other things, the letter stated:

Mr Geary's dismissal was effected by the Commissioner (General Eoin O'Duffy) with the written consent of the Minister for Justice

(Mr James Fitzgerald Kenney SC) pursuant to Section 24 of the Garda Síochána Disciplinary [sic] Regulations 1926 … Having regard to the fact that in later years evidence was 'cooked' by the IRA to discredit Ministers, Deputies, etc. etc. it is not beyond the bounds of possibility or even probability that the evidence against Superintendent Geary was 'cooked'.[1]

It defies logic that the Department of Justice should have quoted Section 24 which clearly could not, legally, have been applied to Superintendent William Geary. Under Section 24 the commissioner, in exercising the powers conferred on him 'to dismiss from the Force any member (not being an officer) whom he considers unfit for retention', could not have dismissed William, as he was an officer.[2]

In 1970 a friend, Danny O'Connor from Tournafulla, invited William to go to watch the Gaelic games in Gaelic Park in the Bronx. On the way home Danny mentioned that he had a copy of David Neligan's book *The Spy in the Castle*.[3] William borrowed this book and subsequently wrote to Neligan to congratulate him. This started an exchange of gracious letters between the two men during 1971.[4] In closing, Neligan invariably used a friendly phrase such as 'Sincere good wishes', or 'Affectionately'. In a letter of 11 June 1971, Neligan said, 'I accept unquestionably that you never received money.' In December 1971 he promised that he would clear William's name: 'I can do nothing until the Minister for Justice makes a move … if he does, I am prepared to make a statement clearing you as it is fairly clear to me now that you never received that money.' He had many unavailedof opportunities to make a statement clearing William Geary's name. One minister even suggested that he would give immunity to him under the Official Secrets Act. Neligan stonewalled, however, possibly because he considered that such a move would leave him vulnerable to prosecution or legal civil claim.

The friendliness and openness of the exchanges proved illusory when Neligan had to address the Geary question in other forums where he adopted an exculpatory stance. Here is part of his handwritten statement on 14 October 1972 to the Department of Justice:

> In 1928, when I was Chief of the Detective Br G.S., information came in that William Geary G.S. had received £100 from the IRA for working for them. This was from an unimpeachable source, the origin of which I am not at liberty to disclose.
>
> The Supt was dismissed by the Government. Mr Geary denies that he ever received any money and that he ever had any dealings with those persons. That may well be: only he and the IRA Chiefs at the time can answer the question. This affair has rankled with Mr Geary ever since, doubtless rightly.
>
> Some time ago I wrote to the Sec. Dept of Justice about the matter and got no reply.
>
> So long a time has elapsed that it is difficult to see what can be done now.[5]

This statement equates the IRA with an 'unimpeachable source' (the only source in all the records and correspondence is the coded letter from the IRA): how could the garda head of security truthfully say that the IRA could not be accused of treason against the Free State? It is nonsensical to suggest, as he does in the phrase 'the origin of which I am not at liberty to disclose', that the ex-garda security chief could not confide in the Minister for Justice. It appears that the phrases 'That may well be' and 'doubtless rightly' were a concession to what he believed to be the truth.

William continued his quest to have his dismissal rescinded, approaching a later Minister for Justice, Gerard (Gerry) Collins, TD. Collins wrote to Neligan on 20 December 1977, stating:

Mr Geary has forwarded copies of two letters, dated 30 December 1971 and 14 October 1972, which he received from you. In the course of your letter of 30 December you say, 'I can do nothing until the Minister for Justice makes a move. If he does, I am prepared to make a statement clearing you as it is fairly clear to me now that you never received that money.'

I am now looking into the case and would be glad if you would let me know whether you would be prepared to make a statement on the lines of that you indicated in your letter to Mr Geary, together with any information that might be of assistance in reviewing the matter.

Incidentally, you say in your letter of 14 October 1972, that you wrote to the Secretary, Department of Justice but got no reply. No record of the receipt of such a letter can be traced.[6]

Neligan's response on the following day was a curt scribbled note:

Dear Sir

I have your letter of the 20 inst.

This Geary Business is an enigma which I cannot solve.

In the circs there is nothing I can do.

Yours etc.

D. Neligan[7]

This exchange shows Neligan's duplicity and the bureaucratic manoeuvring of the government in response to William's initiative.

In December 1977 William decided to submit to a 'lie detector test'. He was able to arrange this through his godson and friend John Patrick Collins, who was a judge in Manhattan at the time – his mother, Susan McAuliffe, had been William's school companion in Ballyagran. The summation of the polygraph examination on 20 December 1977 is as follows:

Based upon the information supplied, the polygraph test interview, the analysis of the emotional reactions recorded on the polygraph charts to the above pertinent test questions and an intensive post-test interrogation of Mr Geary, it is my professional OPINION that the subject's answers to the above pertinent test questions were TRUTHFUL and that he did not take 100 pounds from anyone on behalf of the Irish Republicans or anyone else to provide them with secret information.

Respectfully submitted,

Nat Laurendi

Polygraphist, Academy of Certified Polygraphists[8]

William forwarded the results to Minister for Justice Gerry Collins on 23 December 1977. On 31 May 1978, Collins wrote to William explaining his exhaustive work to try to resolve the issues, saying, 'Everything that is available (including press cuttings, etc.) has been submitted to and considered by the attorney general as well as being considered by me', and, 'There are no official documents available to show why you were dismissed although thorough searches have been made, and in fact the information that you were accused of involvement with the IRA has come entirely from you. The only official record is the record of the decision dismissing you.'[9]

This assertion was inaccurate because at that time, and from 26 June 1928 up to and including December 2009, four relevant documents germane to the minister's assertion were on file, although not available to the public until 2002. These four documents were:

1   The photograph of the coded IRA letter purporting to incriminate William Geary.

2   The six-page tightly typed foolscap pages of Neligan's accusatory report, dated 20 June 1928.

3   The four pages of typed foolscap by Commissioner O'Duffy, dated 20 June 1928, endorsing Neligan's report and stating that 'the Superintendent is guilty of treachery, and I recommend that he be dismissed from the Force with ignominy forthwith'.

4   William Geary's official request dated 19 June 1928 for permission to engage a solicitor in accordance with Routine Order C.241, August 1927.

Collins also said:

> It is not possible to decide that a dismissal of 50 years ago
> was unjustified or even that the matter was open to doubt just
> because the information on which the authorities acted is not
> now available to be evaluated … the evidence on which they were
> based has, in the normal process, been lost through the periodic
> pulping of old files.[10]

In reply William Geary protested about 'built in bureaucratic
resistance'. On 12 July 1978 came the reply of the minister's
private secretary Dermot Cole: 'You misunderstood the
Minister's reference to the pulping of files and the Minister
made no such reference as you attribute to him.'[11] The private
secretary followed up with some additional explanations:

> The minister does not think he can add much substance to
> what he said … Mr Neligan told you in a letter of 14 October
> 1972 that he had written a letter on some unspecified date, to
> the Department of Justice on your behalf. I am to state that no
> such letter has been found … there is no question of any 'built in
> bureaucratic resistance' …[12]

However, William was tenacious in his pursuit of justice. In a
letter to 'The Honourable Gerard Collins TD' acknowledging
a letter from Dermot Cole, he quotes Collins' private secretary,
'that you shall rescind my dismissal from the Garda Síochána if
the necessary evidence is forthcoming … I shall appreciate your

advising me as to what you consider to be necessary evidence to give a basis for action'.[13]

This letter was sent a couple of months after Commissioner Edmund Garvey successfully challenged the state in the Supreme Court for unlawful dismissal. Garvey joined the force in 1939; he was a distinguished detective and was renowned for his organisational ability; he was honoured by the Dutch government for his rescue of Dr Tiede Herrema, a Dutch businessman kidnapped in Limerick by members of the Provisional IRA; and he was a strict disciplinarian. He was appointed commissioner in September 1975 and was sacked by the Fianna Fáil government of Jack Lynch in 1978. He won a legal challenge for unfair dismissal, which was later upheld by the Supreme Court. The government had to pass the Garda Síochána Act 1979 to validate the actions of his successor.

But Gerry Collins continued to pursue the matter in another direction. A letter of 2 August 1978 to David Neligan revealed the 'basis' on which he hoped the matter could be successfully concluded:

Dear Mr Neligan,

I am sorry to bother you again about the case of Mr William Geary, a former Superintendent of the Garda Síochána but I now have received a copy of a letter from Mr Geary which you wrote to him on 29 (or 27) July 1971 which I had not heard of in detail before (copy attached).

I should be grateful if you would indicate to me, now, what information or representations you intended to convey to the Department of Justice when, as stated in your letter of 29 July, 1971, you had sought an interview with the Department concerning Mr Geary. (No record can be found in the Department of such a request from you at the time.)

It has been suggested in public comment that perhaps you may be concerned lest the disclosure of information in your possession about this case might be an offence under the Official Secrets Act, 1963. May I therefore explain that the prohibition in that Act (Section 4) on the communication of official information does not apply where the person concerned is duly authorised by a Minister. This is explicitly provided for in the Act. Accordingly, as Minister for Justice, I am now, by this letter, formally authorising you, as well as requesting you, to disclose to me any information which you may have that might show or suggest that Mr Geary was wrongfully dismissed.

Yours sincerely Gerard Collins, TD,

Minister for Justice[14]

Clearly the minister was seeking new evidence from Neligan to form a basis for wrongful dismissal. This could bypass the initial denial of due process by Commissioner O'Duffy, Minister of Justice Kenney and President William T. Cosgrave in 1928. It would also obviate the need to examine the bureaucratic bungling from 1928 onward.

In a reply to Collins' letter of 2 August 1978 and dated the next day, Neligan sent a scribbled, handwritten, almost illegible note to the Department of Justice. It cleverly avoided the minister's invitation to absorb blame, encouraged the minister to find other grounds to see justice done, and invited sympathy for Neligan's old age:

Booterstown County Dublin

Dear Mr Collins

I have yr lr. of 2 inst … I have arrived at the conclusion that Geary has suffered enough & should be pardoned.

You can make any use of this letter that you think fit.

About my lr to Justice in 1971 – someone is lying & that someone is <u>not</u> me.

Excuse bad writing – cause: old age!

Yours etc.

D. Neligan[15]

The minister's secretary wrote to William on 17 August 1978 confirming that he had written to Neligan requesting disclosure of information and that Neligan had supplied no information. He finished by saying 'the Minister regrets that he is unable to be of further assistance in the matter …'

But the collapse of the efforts to obtain justice did not deter William. Six years later, on 20 August 1984, William wrote to the then Minister for Justice, Michael Noonan, TD. In the course of the letter he said, 'As Mr Collins did not deem the letters adequate to act favourably on my behalf, I submitted to a polygraph examination and sent the report to him on 23 December 1977.'[16] All William ever wished for was to have his honour restored, and he submitted a sworn affidavit before a notary public in which he wrote: 'Without any reservation I want the record to show that in the event of my being granted exoneration by the Republic of Ireland, I waive all rights to back pay and any compensation whatsoever as all I want is to have my name cleared.'[17]

One of the ways in which William continued his quest was to work with Frank Prendergast, TD, Limerick. On 11 December 1984 the research officer of the Labour Party wrote to Prendergast and disclosed the existence of a file marked 'Dismissals', for the period 16 May 1925 to 2 May 1932. This file, under the sub-heading S 9051, contained reference to William Geary and was designated as 'not available to the public until AD 2002'.[18]

At about this time William's wife Margaret became very ill with multiple sclerosis. Initially she was cared for at home, but eventually she had to go to a nursing home. William devotedly went there daily to care for her until her death on 2 February 1985.

It was not until 26 March 1987 that he wrote to former Minister of Justice Collins again:

No doubt you remember the case very well having made a thorough investigation in 1978. In your letter, 31 May 1978, it was stated that the main impediment to resolve the case in my favour was the absence of any official documentation.

It came as a shock to me when the Labour Party Research Office, Leinster House, Dublin 2 disclosed that the file in my case with others of the period 16.5.1925–2.5.1932, marked

'DISMISSALS' exists, but [is] not available for public reading until the year 2002. The research was initiated by Mr Frank Prendergast, TD, Limerick …

To me at my age the acquisition of money as compensation for the stigma I had to bear all these years I do not covet. Therefore, I have made an affidavit to that effect.

Sincerely yours

William Geary[19]

8

FORCES FOR NATURAL JUSTICE

William's sociability gave him deep roots in the Irish community in New York and the Bronx. One such connection was as godfather to Judge John Patrick Collins. In December 1990 Judge Collins requested access to the 'Dismissals' file William had heard about from the Labour Party Research Office. On 14 August 1990, in a reply to Judge Collins, Mr P. Connolly of the National Archives advised that the file (S 9051) was held at his office. He said, 'Its status will be reviewed before the end of 1990, but given the status of the file, it may remain closed after that', and advised that the decision about access lay with the certifying officer, Department of the Taoiseach, under the National Archives Act 1986, and that if the file was closed to inspection, this position would be reviewed every five years.[1]

On 22 October 1990 William appealed in a letter to the Taoiseach, Charles J. Haughey, TD, for access to file S 9051. His letter was acknowledged on 13 November 1990 and the correspondence was passed to Ray Burke, TD, Minister for Justice.

On 3 December 1990, Mary Robinson was inaugurated as President of Ireland. Before her election to the presidency, as an academic, senator and barrister she had sought to use law as an instrument for social change. She had argued landmark cases before the European Court of Human Rights. It is doubtless that, given Robinson's reputation, William saw her inauguration as an opportunity in the quest to clear his name, since his unjust dismissal was a violation of his civil rights. On 12 April 1991 he wrote to President Mary Robinson at Áras an Uachtaráin:

Your Excellency:

Reports indicate that you hate injustice and became involved in unpopular causes, so I write to you in confidence that you can help me undo the injustice inflicted on me, sixty-three years ago.

I was dismissed from the Garda Síochána (A Superintendent) 26 June, 1928, by the Executive Council, Irish Free State, without a trial on the allegation that I accepted a bribe of £100.0.0 from the Republicans. I took no bribe nor was I offered one.

My last effort to clear my name was when I wrote to Mr Charles J. Haughey, Taoiseach, 22 October 1990, who acknowledged the letter, a copy of which is enclosed with the papers in the case.

Unmerited disgrace has been my lot. Considering my age (92) I am most anxious to have the blemish on my name removed and for your help I shall be deeply grateful.

Sincerely

William Geary[2]

Robinson's secretary replied:

> Oifig Rúnaí an Uachtaráin Baile Atha Cliath 8
> 25 April 1991
>
> Dear Mr Geary
> Thank you for your letter of 12 April, 1991, addressed to the President, Mary Robinson, concerning your dismissal from the Garda Síochána in 1928.
>
> The President very much regrets that it is not possible for her to intervene as you request. She is arranging to have your letter referred to the appropriate Government authority for attention.
>
> Yours sincerely,
> Peter Ryan
> Secretary to the President[3]

William had further discouragement in a letter dated 3 May 1991 from the private secretary to the Minister for Justice, Ray Burke, TD, who advised:

> As you will recall, the only file available on your dismissal from the Force when you last corresponded with the then Minister for Justice, Mr Gerard Collins TD, contained nothing more than a formal record of the decision to dismiss – there was no official documentation available as to the background … The file does not contain anything that helps your case … In the circumstances, it is not considered that anything useful would be gained by releasing this file to the National Archives.[4]

William made a further appeal, offering more evidence, to Burke on 11 June 1991. This was formally acknowledged on 24 June, and he wrote again in August offering additional evidence to the minister. He received a perfunctory acknowledgement. Given the politics of the day, Mr Burke's indifference to William's appeal for justice does not come as a surprise.

In 1992 Fr Thomas Killian Carroll, DD, became acquainted with William while ministering in New York.[5] Fr Carroll's father was a member of the Garda Síochána and was the clerical officer in the district office in Longford, which undoubtedly added a measure of empathy to their flourishing friendship. On 20 November 1992, William gave a typed résumé of his life to Carroll, who approached Albert Reynolds, TD. Reynolds was known to the Carroll family and was about to become Taoiseach. This appeal seems not to have borne fruit, probably due to cabinet chaos at that time.[6]

However, Fr Tom Carroll believed William to be the victim of a grievous injustice and continued his efforts to see justice done. He contacted his relative, John Wilson, TD, who served in Dáil Éireann for nineteen years in seven ministerial posts and as Tanaiste. However, this attempt to obtain a hearing suffered the same fate as the effort previously addressed to Minister for Justice Ray Burke.

In September 1998 Judge John P. Collins once again requested access to the closed file on behalf of William, this time under the Freedom of Information Act 1997. Legally, a person is entitled to access his or her personal files, but this was not granted.[7] After some time Peter Ryan, of the Taoiseach's department, wrote to Collins saying, 'There are two records on file S 9051 that concern Mr Geary and copies of these records are attached'; these included redacted copies of the statements of Eoin O'Duffy and David Neligan made on 20 June 1928, plus other notes and an indecipherable copy of the coded IRA message and what purported to be a translation.

As had been the case with Neligan's *The Spy in the Castle*, once again a publication by a former member of the Garda Síochána came to be significant in Geary's journey to vindication. Tim Leahy, a man of many distinctions, published his memoirs in December 1996.[8] The book was a huge success, having been lauded by John B. Keane – poet, novelist, essayist and ballad writer – and having received a glowing accolade from Conor Brady, editor of *The Irish Times*.[9] A second edition was printed in April 1997.

On 5 September 1998 William wrote to Tim Leahy saying, 'My godson, John Patrick Collins, Justice of the Supreme Court of the State of New York, sent me a copy of your book *Memoirs of a Garda Superintendent*.'[10] William's letter was accompanied by a short autobiography. Leahy replied on 18 September 1998, and on 28 September William's response says, 'Really, I am very pleased that you think the enclosures I sent you would be of interest for publication in the *Garda Review*, to which I have no objection. The idea is excellent. You have my thanks.'[11]

Leahy also had other ideas and on 12 October 1998 wrote to Conor Brady, editor of *The Irish Times*, sending him copies of the correspondence with William Geary and expressing a wish that it might be published in the newspaper. Before replying to Leahy, Brady took action on several fronts. In a reply on 20 October he thanked Leahy and remarked, 'Mr Geary would have been a superintendent in Kilrush while his late father was superintendent in Ballyvaughan.' He went on to say that he had talked with David Neligan, who had admitted that the evidence against Geary was tenuous. He speculated that he could persuade Commissioner Pat Byrne to look at the file, hoping to see if William had been wrongly accused. In deference to William's advanced years, he expressed the view that it would be a good thing to clear his name while 'he was still with us'. He suggested that the *Garda Review* give the story the 'full treatment' and that he could send a reporter to interview William. At that point he shrewdly expressed caution and concern: 'What I wouldn't want to do, though, is pursue the file and then find that he's plainly and incontrovertibly guilty. It wouldn't do any good at the closing of his days to have that final humiliation – what good would that do anyone?'[12]

The Brady–Leahy axis was beginning to have results, and on 10 December 1998 William wrote:

Dear Tim,

Your letter of 3 December with the paper clipping came yesterday and I wish to thank you for the brilliant idea of sending my file to Mr Conor Brady, *Irish Times*, a man of action, whose celerity we must admire, as I was interviewed by Margaret Ward on 23 and 30 November.[13]

Brady intimated that he knew former minister Gerry Collins very well and would discuss the case with him. On 4 January 1999 Leahy wrote to Brady about Margaret Ward's interview, saying, 'he was thrilled with this development, this may be the wedge to pierce the bureaucratic shield'.[14] It was likely that William, though 'thrilled', was still mindful of the possibility that the indifference displayed in 1928 by William T. Cosgrave's administration regarding the administration of justice, which had continued to pervade all the exchanges between him and the state, might still persist.

The Irish Times of 23 January 1999 included a news feature by journalist Margaret Ward; it was a concise and masterful presentation of all the salient facts about William Geary. Ward's research was thorough and penetrated into the Taoiseach's office and the Department of Justice. Publicity was beginning to scorch a path into the public mind, and Ward reported:

> However, this week it appeared that, finally, there was a light at the end of the tunnel. Following queries by *The Irish Times*, the Taoiseach's office said it was releasing Mr Geary's dismissal notice to his godson, Judge John Collins of New York.[15]

Another feature in *The Irish Times* of 23 January 1999, under a banner heading 'Superintendent's dismissal clearly invalid', contained a thought-provoking legal analysis of the procedures employed to dismiss Superintendent William Geary. Written by Professor Dermot Walsh, director of the Centre for

Criminal Justice at the University of Limerick, it was a gripping exposition of all the legal elements surrounding the events in June 1928:

> The consequences of a failure to follow the principles of natural justice in dismissing Geary from the force are that his dismissal was unlawful, null and void ... The invalidity of his dismissal does not depend on a formal ruling by the court to that effect. It follows directly and automatically from the failure to comply with the principles of natural justice.[16]

Three days after Margaret Ward's feature appeared, a letter from Catherine Byrne, Department of Justice, Equality and Law Reform, addressed to Mr John P. Collins, proposed to make the Geary file available to him. The following points are worth revisiting:

1   Under Irish Common Law a person is innocent until proven guilty.

2   Despite O'Duffy's stated belief that his officer 'deserves capital punishment', there was no arrest, charge, or caution, which the law requires when grave charges are being preferred. Consequently the highly charged conversation in Carmody's Hotel in Kilrush in the presence of Commissioner O'Duffy, Deputy Commissioner Coogan and Chief Superintendent Neligan would not be admissible in evidence.

3   William Geary's statutory rights to a sworn enquiry, conferred on him by the Garda Síochána (Discipline) Regulations 1926

issued by Minister for Justice Kevin O'Higgins on 1 May 1926, were denied to him.

4   In his written request on 19 June 1928 for a solicitor to assist in his defence, William Geary was complying with Routine Order C.241 of August 1927. In neglecting to respond, Commissioner O'Duffy failed in his sworn duty, and he could hardly plead ignorance because he was the person who issued the Routine Orders eight months previously.

In February 1999 *The Irish Times* followed the Geary article with revelations that influenced public opinion and put pressure on the bureaucracy.[17] The revelations covered the infamous fatal ambush of the National Army at Knocknagoshel in 1923, when the IRA lured them into a trap by describing an arms dump in a letter which it knew would be intercepted by the state's intelligence. Quoting Peadar O'Donnell, a former member of the IRA Army Council, the article in *The Irish Times* suggested that a similar postal ploy had been devised by Seán MacBride, the IRA chief of staff, who, it was claimed some years after the events, resisted a suggestion to execute Geary; T. J. Ryan, the officer commanding the Kilrush IRA, implemented the plan. Margaret Ward, having analysed copies of William Geary's file, also reported in the article:

The main evidence against him is in two intercepted IRA letters with encoded messages.

The first is correspondence between the IRA's OC West Clare Battalion and the director of intelligence. The deciphered message reads: 'Arrange with Geary to continue the raids on houses and keep him supplied with lists of places to be raided. Hostile publicity will be continued.'

The second, a badly photocopied document, or photo, is completely illegible except for a decoded message reading:

'Have handed over the hundred pounds to Superintendent Geary. He was very satisfied with the amount. I have given him list of houses which can be safely raided from time to time. It would be well to hit up Geary as hard as possible in An Phoelacht (sic) as he is working satisfactory. Let me know if I may drop the other C.I.D. Have sent on by courier the latest stuff as it is important you should have it at once.'[18]

After two months had elapsed William's elation began to subside; he wrote to Tim Leahy on 29 March 1999 saying: 'John Collins tells me *The Irish Times* is of opinion the Minister for Justice intends to delay action in my case, since pressure has died down, and that I should take legal action now. He suggests I drop you a note to obtain your thinking on the matter.'[19] Leahy replied suggesting that the restoration of the rank of superintendent for William was expected on St Patrick's Day (17 March). He further stated:

… he had been in touch with Conor Brady who said that the Attorney General, whom he knows, had mentioned it to the Minister for Justice, John O'Donoghue, who was to bring the matter before the Cabinet for consideration; apparently it has not been done yet … We both agreed that if no decision is given within say three weeks you should consider putting the government on notice that you propose instituting proceedings by way of judicial review by the High Court. Conor told me that at least two Barristers were volunteering to act on your behalf free of charge … It would of course be far more preferable if this unfortunate matter were amicably settled without recourse to litigation. We suggest as stated that you wait another three weeks when the issue may be reconsidered.[20]

The Irish Times returned to the fray on 13 April 1999 and in a strongly worded editorial implied the imminence of positive action by the government. It described briefly the history of the William Geary case, stating that the relevant files released to him showed serious and obvious inconsistencies in the case assembled by his superiors at the time. The editorial quoted the case of Commissioner Edmund Garvey, dismissed in 1977, who was later vindicated in the Supreme Court by a majority of four to one, showing that in his dismissal he was denied natural justice. The last paragraph illustrated William's magnanimity as well as the critical necessity of addressing the issue if the government wished to retain any credibility:

Mr Geary has been reluctant to take the legal route. He wishes to have no dispute with the Government or to become embroiled in proceedings. He has waived his rights to monetary compensation, beyond seeking the return of monies which he contributed to his pension fund between 1922 and 1928. It is to be hoped therefore that Mr O'Donoghue's recommendation to the Cabinet will not fall short of a complete restoration of Mr Geary's honour and an unqualified acknowledgement that the case made against him in 1928 was spurious. It would be wrong to make a man of Mr Geary's years go to the courts. If he is compelled to do so he undoubtedly will. And there can be little, if any, doubt as to what the outcome would be. A frank acknowledgement that an injustice was done in 1928 would be both generous and pragmatic.[21]

On 21 April 1999 the seventy-year-long train of events culminated in a letter from Minister for Justice, Equality and Law Reform John O'Donoghue to William Geary. In it O'Donoghue stated that he was making a public statement concerning the government's decision on the preceding day to exonerate William unreservedly, and that the government was making an *ex gratia* payment of £50,000 and restoring his full pension rights.

William had never had a case to answer, as confirmed in O'Donoghue's letter, in the final paragraph of which he clarified the situation:

Finally, with regard to the question of granting a Pardon, which has been the subject of some speculation, the Minister wishes to make it clear that Mr. Geary was never charged with or convicted of any offence in connection with the matters which led to his dismissal from the Force in 1928. Accordingly, the question of a Pardon, which only applies to cases where a punishment has been imposed by a Court exercising criminal jurisdiction, does not arise.[22]

On 30 May 1999 Leahy addressed a letter to William, expecting that, now that William's honour had been restored, he would be prepared to make a visit to Ireland after seventy-one years of self-imposed exile. William would no longer have to exclaim, 'Anyway, I was damned as a traitor.' Leahy wrote:

> I have perused and tried to analyse the intercepted IRA letters. One thing that strikes me is that as a Superintendent in the area you would be aware of the interception of these dispatches and surely if you were in cahoots with them you would have warned them not in any circumstances mention your name or give any hint of the liaison. Yet your name is mentioned openly. Again the Director of Intelligence refers to the need for extreme care in correspondence and at the same time takes no care in dealings as between him and the West Clare Battalion O/C. Sounds very fishy. Keep me advised of the date of your visit.
>
> With best wishes
>
> Tim Leahy[23]

The saga of William Geary's fight for justice is a David-and-Goliath one. After his ordeal at the depot headquarters, he had been offered a civil-service post if he confessed and cooperated with the enquiry. William had spurned this offer. He had no ambition to have his name cleared on a legal technicality; he wanted to have his good name publicly restored. The ending of this saga is best articulated by William himself, shortly after he heard the good news:

At this hour of triumph I have to be wary, not to be carried away, or gloat …

I cannot understand why God has singled me out for such an eventful life, given me excellent health, even now at 100 years of age, and while I have been humbled He has given me so much to be grateful for …

I admire the present Irish Government who had the courage to set aside previous adverse decisions, render justice to me long delayed, in particular my good name. In this regard, I want to thank Mr Bertie Ahern, TD, Taoiseach, and Mr John O'Donoghue, TD, Minister for Justice for their initiative, whose names shall go down in history.

Despite what happened to me there, I still have a deep affection for the people of West Clare, where I spent two happy years, in Kilrush.

Finally I take this opportunity to thank each and every one who called to congratulate me on my rehabilitation.

Sincerely

William Geary

Bayside, N.Y.

25 April 1999[24]

AFTERWORD

Shortly after his vindication in April 1999 William wrote to his friend Tim Leahy:

> Now that things have quieted down a bit I am writing to thank you for your phone calls to congratulate me on the very satisfactory outcome of my fight for justice and also to have your opinion as to which factor influenced the Government to act favourably when you take into account previous indifference ... Really I am most grateful to the Government for being so gracious and I am quite satisfied, above all that my reputation is restored ... I would say that since my dismissal was illegal, not according to due process, and the possibility of a legal battle, the Government thought it prudent to settle the matter.[1]

The Irish Times celebrated the victory in an editorial headlined 'Fair Play at Last', two days after the government announcement. It outlined the terms of the settlement offered, and it quoted John O'Donoghue, saying:

> The Minister also declared that in his view 'the procedures that led to his dismissal in 1928 were not satisfactory and that if they were followed today would not be regarded as being in conformity

with the requirements of natural justice as currently understood. The Government considers it reasonable,' the Minister said, 'that Mr Geary's good name and reputation should be restored and that this should be given recognition in a practical way.'[2]

Remarkably John O'Donoghue, TD, was the one Minister of Justice William had not appealed to directly. In a subsequent visit to New York to confirm the Irish government's $15,000 yearly donation to the Jerry McCabe Fellowship Programme, O'Donoghue took the opportunity to invite William to lunch and to offer his personal congratulations.[3] The meeting took place on 15 November 1999 in Rosie O'Grady's Restaurant in Manhattan. William's daughter, Helen Geary Markett, and his godson, Judge Collins, accompanied him.

The Irish newspapers covered the meeting and ceremony.[4] According to Margaret Ward's account:

> Mr O'Donoghue made an announcement clearing Mr Geary's name and restoring his honour in April despite strong opposition from within the Department of Justice and the precedent set by former governments. Mr Geary was also awarded $67,500 (*ex gratia*).
>
> The Minister's request for a meeting was 'the most gracious thing,' said Mr Geary. 'I was very surprised and never expected it although I always wanted to thank the Minister in person.'
>
> The Minister expressed his tremendous admiration for Mr Geary. 'Mr Geary's story epitomises the unquenchable thirst of the human spirit for justice … It's about a man's determination, commitment and burning desire to clear his name.'[5]

William Geary – in his private life, in his pursuit of justice, and in his victory – showed himself as a man of the highest integrity: gentle, resolute, generous and forgiving. His merits were recognised on 15 September 2000 when Reverend James Moynihan, bishop of Syracuse, NY, conferred on him a knighthood in the Equestrian Order of the Holy Sepulchre in Jerusalem. This Catholic chivalric order traces its origins back to Godfrey of Bouillon, principal leader of the First Crusade.

William's self-imposed exile from Ireland was to end when his honour was restored. Tentative arrangements for a return visit were made, but petered out due to age, health, family and social concerns. His advanced age did not impair his mental agility, as is evidenced by his letter-writing, including his correspondence with the *IPA Journal*, and the interviews he conducted with journalists. His hobby – carving walking sticks, one of which he gave me on 13 August 2003 – attested to his interest in the most fitting physical exercise for a man who by then had lived to see the turn of two centuries. William's advice to gardaí is best propounded in extracts from a letter from him to the *IPA Journal*:

The performance of duty well done has its own reward and requires courage, fortitude, dedication and to be conscious that you uphold the dignity of the State and the safety of the people – the alternative is chaos.

My message to you is to wear the uniform with pride and serve with honour – guardians of the peace, unshakeable pillars of justice – in a world often unaware of your great contribution to the wellbeing of society.[6]

William's inability to travel to Ireland was regrettable, not least because receptions were planned for him in Limerick, Ballyagran and Kilrush, and by the garda commissioner and, especially, Assistant Commissioner Hickey, who communicated regularly with former superintendent Tim Leahy.

William died on 17 October 2004 after a short illness, having contracted pneumonia. His daughters Helen Geary Markett and Anne Geary Wallace, and his godson Judge John P. Collins, mourned his death. His death marked the passing of the last remaining original member of the Garda Síochána. William's obituary in *The Irish Times* was accompanied by a picture with the caption 'William Geary: a dapper man, with a fondness for bow ties, white shirts, tweed caps and walking canes'.[7] In the *IPA Journal*, I, the journal's editor, wrote the following tribute to William Geary:

> With extreme sadness I must inform readers of *IPA Journal* that our dear friend and regular correspondent, William Geary, has passed to his eternal reward. He was in his 106th year, had lived in three centuries and was communicating with his many friends right up to his demise.[8]

William's obituary in *Catholic New York* in November 2004 read:

> William Geary, a former Irish policeman who spent 71 years trying to clear his name of a bribery charge and finally succeeded at age 100, died Oct. 14 at a hospital in Queens, it was reported.

He was 105. A memorial mass was scheduled for Sunday, Nov. 7, at his former parish church, St John the Evangelist in Manhattan, where he had been a daily communicant ... In 2000, Mr Geary was invested as a Knight of the Holy Sepulchre. Burial was at Calvary Cemetery in Queens. Mr Geary was predeceased by his wife, Margaret Shryane Geary. He is survived by his daughters, Helen Markett and Anne Wallace.

On Sunday 21 November 2004 a memorial holy mass was celebrated in St Michael's Church, Ballyagran, by Reverend Fr Joseph Shire. A large congregation of officials, friends, and family from as far away as New York testified to their respect and affection for William Geary.

Appendix 1:
William's 'Letter re
Engaging of Solicitor'

Below is William's 'Letter re engaging of Solicitor':

PHOENIX PARK DEPOT
DUBLIN
19.6.28

<u>CONFIDENTIAL</u>

The Adjutant,
Depot

Re engaging of Solicitor – Supt. W. Geary,
R.O. C.241, August, 1928

On the 16th June, 1928, at Ennis, I was severely interrogated by the Commissioner, Deputy Commissioner Coogan, Chief Superintendent Neligan, 'S' Branch, and Chief Superintendent O'Duffy, Ennis, regarding a very serious offence which I then strenuously denied and still deny. I was then subjected to the indignity of having my person searched and my pocket book and other private correspondence taken from me. In addition my private correspondence was gone into and all my belongings were carefully searched by Chief Superintendent Neligan with necessary assistance. Certain papers were taken from me and also everything relating to my private banking account. Nothing incriminating was found on me as same did not exist at any time, and the question of compensating me for the unfounded charge and indignity of search should, I submit, be considered when my character is cleared as I know it will.

My integrity, character, honour and family has been besmirched by the action of my authorities on the 16th June, 1928, so it is now up to me to protect myself, and to do so I request authority to employ a Solicitor with necessary assistance, who will go into this matter with me. In the circumstances I do not think that my request is unreasonable.

I am appalled at the enormity of the accusation, so much so, that I am unwilling to accept any compromise whatever, but I want to see the thing through to the bitter end, and I fear in defending my honour I cannot spare any persons whoever they may be. In thinking this affair over since the 16th instant, it is fairly evident to me that my authorities have made a very grave mistake, have fallen to a ruse carefully set with the view of getting me out of Kilrush, in addition to ruining my honour, which I place above all, and also have set the extremist section laughing, as undoubtedly they must. In other words the authorities have not got the culprit, and if I may make a suggestion, it might be no harm if the enquiries were continued, for I have no fear as to the outcome of this allegation ultimately. I know the possibility exists that my name may not be now cleared, but at some time it will be realised what a terrible mistake has been made, and I say this without a shadow of doubt no matter what 'evidence' is apparently against me. I have no fear of consequences as my conscience is clear and I have no reason whatever to hold down my head, and the people who now point the finger at me and say 'Traitor' may live to regret it. I am not a traitor and never was, nor any of my family connections either.

As to my work in Kilrush District, I shall have a lot to say when the time comes, but I leave this for the present.

I shall appreciate an early decision as to my request, for I believe that the Commissioner, who is entrusted with the well-being of the force, is only anxious that justice should be done. It is a sound maxim that it is better that two guilty men should escape, than that an innocent one should be convicted.

I now trust that this report is not deemed insubordinate or disrespectful to my authorities as there is nothing further from my mind, but I feel so strongly on this matter that the words I use do not adequately express my feelings.

Submitted please.

W. GEARY
SUPERINTENDENT[1]

APPENDIX 2:
NELIGAN'S REPORT
AND WILLIAM GEARY'S
STATEMENTS IN RESPONSE

NELIGAN'S REPORT

Below is David Neligan's report 'Irregular Papers Implicating Superintendent Geary':

GARDA SÍOCHÁNA

Oifig An Comisinéara,

Baile Átha Cliath

<u>SECRET</u>

C.S. BRANCH,

20th June, '28

Commissioner

IRREGULAR PAPERS IMPLICATING SUPERINTEN-DENT GEARY

I beg to report that the facts of this case are as follows:

On 1st August, '27, a letter addressed to Miss Eily Murray, Kilmurray McMahon, Co. Clare, was returned to the dead letter office, GPO, where it was opened and the contents found to be an 'IRA' despatch. It was then forwarded to the Department of Justice who subsequently forwarded it to this office. Efforts were made to trace the address which it was meant for, and after several communications with Chief Supt., Clare, it was found that the correspondence was intended for T.J. Ryan, 'O/C West Clare Battalion'. A postal warrant was then applied for and all letters going to that address examined by Chief Supt. O'Duffy, Ennis, copies forwarded to this office, and the originals re-posted. That scheme has continued in operation since, up to date.

It was then sought to trace the address in Dublin to which replies to these letters were being forwarded, and, with the help of P.O. officials this was done. The result was that a second postal warrant was applied for and received and the 'IRA' letters from Clare found, examined and sometimes photographed. It was found that this Dublin address was the depot for letters from other parts of the country, including Cork, Galway and Mayo.

For the last two years Scotland Yard has helped us in the decoding of cipher messages. As certain of these letters contained such messages which defied our expert I asked Col. Carter to help, and he consented.

There are a great number of such code messages on our files, but we are here primarily concerned with two.

On 2nd June, '28, the Chief Supt., Clare, reported that a letter had come through to the Clare address. A copy of this and enclosures I have marked 'A'. On 6th June, '28, a letter purporting to be the reply was forwarded by the Dublin sorting office to this office. I have marked it 'B'. I have pasted over each the decoded message to simplify reading. These are the only letters bearing on the Geary case, and I will submit my observations on them:

The letter of 2nd June, '28, was apparently written by the 'Director of Intelligence' after he had seen a 'GHQ Officer', who brought certain official Garda documents from Clare, where he had received them from Ryan, the 'O/C West Clare Battalion', who in turn had received them from his agent in the Garda.

Now this officer was sent down probably as a result of a communication to 'GHQ' by Ryan that he was in touch with a good source of information and required money urgently, for it will be observed that the 'GHQ Officer' handed to Ryan the sum of £100. This letter did not (so far as we know) come through the post, therefore it is safe to assume that it was sent by courier. Now the letter opens by congratulating Ryan on such a useful coup. 'Our principal friend' is undoubtedly Geary, as will be seen at once by reading para. 3 of the letter 'B'. From the sentence – 'If he continues to give us the important stuff' it is clearly to be inferred that he has already given them important documents, or documents that the 'D.I.' regards as important. They are so important that the 'D.I.' fears Geary will think £100 inadequate payment for them. 'I hope he feels satisfied with £100,' he says. 'The agents in Limerick' are next mentioned. Here we are in the dark. It is clear that Ryan is here, too, the guiding influence. Is Geary also responsible for securing these agents? It looks to me as if he is. If not why mention him in the same breath, as it were?

So far the letter presents no clue as to the identity of the 'principal friend'.

Now in para. 2 the 'D.I.' comes to that dark secret, hence he resorts to the cipher to express his words. Geary is to be safeguarded by getting from Ryan lists of houses for 'dud' raids. His authorities will then have no doubt of his active hostility to the 'I.R.A.' As well, the propaganda sheet, *An Phoblacht*, will aid in the good work. 'Geary will there be attacked as a vicious hunter of Republicans. More camouflage.' 'Hostile publicity will be continued.' The inference here is that this publicity was requested either by Ryan of his own volition, or at Geary's request. I am inclined to believe the latter is correct. Publicity of this sort probably appealed to Geary, who knew that such things are noted and weighed by various officials. This was indeed a new use for hostile propaganda, and I believe it is Geary's idea.

The writer having hidden in cipher the name of the spy proceeds again 'in clear'. There follows precautions to be adopted in order that such a valuable agent should not run the risk of being discovered. Excellent precautions these. Could anything further be done along these lines?

The 'D.I.' knew a useful spy when he saw one. All that now remained was to prevent the 'enemy' getting on this track.

In para. 3 we enter new ground. The deduction here is clear. Geary mentioned to Ryan that a 'high official' of his acquaintance in Cork was to be bought, even as he had been. The 'D.I.' tells Ryan he has lost no time in getting hold of this man and that gold has done its work with him. The contemptuous phrase 'He is as mercenary as the rest of them' of course includes Geary, the spy who demanded £100 as the price of this treachery. 'Do not tell your friend' means that although they acted on Geary's advice it is not necessary to entrust him with the knowledge of the result. 'Keep your spies in water-tight compartments' is as true a maxim now as it was in the days of Machiavelli.

In para. 4 we have advice for further precautions. The inference to be drawn from the first sentence is that Ryan has been operating Geary the whole time through an intermediary, and that intermediary is one of the 'political people,' i.e. a member of the F.F. or S.F. organisation. Ryan is exhorted to continue this as an additional safeguard.

The enclosure (marked 'C') is a receipt form for £100 issued by the 'Officer i/c Finance & Accts, I.R.A.' to be initialled by Ryan. This is dated for 1st May, '28, although the covering letter is dated 1st June, '28, the probable explanation being that the cash was expended in the former month and would therefore be included in the finance imprest for that period.

The covering letter from the 'Finance officer' is of little importance. All three papers were enclosed in one envelope and when copied the packet was duly re-posted and reached Ryan 'safely' as he said in his reply. This reply (marked 'B') came through to the Dublin address on 6th June, '28. In para. 1 of that letter he acknowledged the letter of the 1st June, which I have dealt with. Para. 2 mentioned the receipt which was enclosed. Instead of his name Ryan had written thereon the words 'O/C West Clare Bn.' In para. 3 he finds it necessary to resort to the cipher. He tells the 'D.I.' that he has handed over £100 to Superintendent Geary. The 'D.I.' called the man Geary, but Ryan, as if to make things clearer still, gives him his rank. 'He was very satisfied with the amount.' The 'D.I.' is to have no fears that this agent will …

continue the good work. Ryan has in the next sentence made it clear that he complied with the instructions to give Geary 'dud' raids. In the next he further exhorts 'G.H.Q.' to devote plenty of space and vitriolic abuse to Geary's doings in Clare, and the tone clearly infers that this is Geary's own suggestion, as has already been mentioned in report. 'Let me know' etc., I gather to mean that one of the detectives locally (in Clare or Limerick) is acting treacherously, and now the salmon, Geary, is safe on the hook. Ryan does not want to trouble himself with the sprat the D.O. From the last sentence it is clear that Geary has handed over a second lot of official papers, which are regarded (by Ryan) as urgent and important enough to render justifiable and necessary sending them to Dublin. The employment of the courier ensures secrecy and safety.

These are the two letters which implicate Geary; in fact it may be said that they constitute the whole case for the prosecution, as it were.

I set down below some questions that occur to me, and the answers.

(1) Q. Was Geary aware of the fact that these 'I.R.A.' letters were being examined by the police?

A. He was aware of this from the beginning, and that is the most extraordinary feature of the case. One may ask why, if this man was acting treacherously, did he not safeguard himself by informing Ryan that his (Ryan's) correspondence was being tampered with? It is difficult to find an adequate answer. Perhaps he arranged with Ryan that his own name would never appear on 'I.R.A.' documents; that incriminating papers would be sent by hand and every precaution taken to safeguard him from discovery. Also he may have thought that the sudden cease of these letters would make the police authorities suspicious, and for some obscure reason did not tell Ryan. Although I have devoted considerable time and thought to this question I cannot answer it satisfactorily. Is it not a fact that in every crime there is one glaring error? Perhaps the omission to sell this with other secrets is Geary's. Again, a spy does not sell all his secrets at once; when 'trade' is slack would not the tit-bit of the letters fetch another £100?

(2) Q. Were the 'I.R.A.' aware of the letter-censoring?

A. No. It is unlikely that they were, although admittedly the courier precaution, etc., and the wording of the 'D.I.'s' letter go to show that they mistrusted the post to a great extent.

(3) Q. Were they aware that this code could be deciphered by us?

A. No. They had recently changed over to a new and far more difficult code, and it was given out in Court lately that the police could not decode 'I.R.A.' messages.

(4) Q. What are Geary's previous political history and connections?

A. It would appear that he never participated in the Volunteer movement and was an average provincial youth of the farming class. He is not known to have any relatives who are hostile to the State, but enquiry on this is proceeding.

(5) Q. What is his record in the force relative to political matters?

A. He never distinguished himself in this sphere, and was

not known as hostile to the Irregulars; neither was he known or suspected to be a sympathiser with them.

(6) Q. His financial condition?

A. He possesses securities and shares worth approximately £300, and is not known to be in debt.

(7) Q. His known character?

A. He was believed to be of good, sober habits, but a search of his rooms disclosed a quantity of pornographic literature, formulae for aphrodisiacs, anti-venereal outfit and chemicals. He had apparently become familiar with these devices during his service at sea, he being an ex-wireless operator of the merchant service. It is not without significance that Ryan is also an ex-wireless operator.

(8) Q. His ability as an Officer?

A. I believe he was regarded as fairly efficient, although he did not distinguish himself in the Roscrea bank robbery case.

(9) Q. Is there a possibility that this is a diabolical plot to ruin Geary?

A. While anything is possible this cannot be ruled out, but I do think that it is so remote as to be unworthy of serious consideration. I have never heard of such a plot, and it is far too clever to be true. To what end would it be done? It is outside the pale of likely contingencies.

(10) Q. Would the 'I.R.A.' have reason to seek doing Geary a grave injury?

A. I do not see why they should. He has never, to my knowledge, done them any harm; no Irregular has suffered through his efforts; he took no part in the civil strife, and they cannot have any serious grievance against him.

(11) Q. Is it a fact that Geary was attacked in *An Phoblacht*?

A. Yes. For months past he has been mentioned in that paper mostly in connection with raids on Republican houses, and I must say that it struck me as peculiar that so much raiding was going on in the district. In my view Geary's guilt explains this frenzy of raiding adequately. The letters stress it beyond doubt.

(12) Q. Is it a fact that he carried out more raids than the average Supt.?

A. Yes. In fact his principal anti-Irregular activity seemed to consist of raiding and nothing else.

(13) Q. What is the net result of these political raids? (i) in prisoners (ii) in captured war material.

A. Nil.

(14) Q. Did the Supt. accuse members of his district force with loose talking on official matters?

A. Yes. About three months ago he accused, in a general way, the detectives in his district, of loose talking. They protested to the Commissioner as a result.

(15) Q. What is thought to be the object of this?

A. To enable him to say afterwards if a leakage came to the ears of the authorities, 'I told you so,' and point the finger of suspicion at the detectives, and incidentally away from himself. He may also have thought that the detectives were beginning to suspect something in the wind, and he may have decided that the best form of defence is attack. If, afterwards, they charged him with loose talking or something more serious, he would naturally direct attention to the fact of his having charged them (which charge was made before members of the uniform force), and say they bore a grudge against him.

(16) Q. On being confronted with the treachery charge did he state that he suspected some person in his district force of being the traitor?

A. Yes. He said that his clerk, Garda Corbett, was an Irregular prior to joining the force, and suggested that he may still be in touch with them. He said that he had only received this information a few days previously.

(17) Q. Are there any grounds for this allegation?

A. None. I believe from the Garda's history and demeanour that he is innocent of the charge. I believe it is a subterfuge of Geary to throw the blame on other shoulders.

(18) Q. Did Geary report his suspicion concerning the clerk when he heard about the letter 'A'?

A. No. Although he had several days in which to do so, he never communicated his suspicions to any person, though he discussed with D.O. Keyes members likely to part with information.

(19) Q. When did Geary become aware that the letter 'A' had been found?

A. On the day it was found he was told by D.O. Keyes of its contents. Of course the decoded portion was not then available.

(20) Q. What observation is he alleged to have made to D.O. Keyes on being told of the letter 'A'?

A. According to D.O. Keyes he said 'Sure they'll never find the name,' or words to that effect. He meant the name of the traitor of course.

(21) Q. Did Geary consult his Chief Superintendent when he heard that base treachery was going on in the force under his

immediate control?

A. No. Although he had several days to do so.

(22) Q. Did Geary, after his transfer to Co. Clare, report that his car had been maliciously damaged and did he receive compensation?

A. Yes. With the object probably of getting out of the division, or showing that his life was in danger.

(23) Q. Was Geary surprised when he heard the charge?

A. Probably not. His knowledge of the finding of the letter forearmed him, or he had no reason to believe his name would be mentioned, or that the code would be deciphered. In fact it is fairly certain that Ryan assured him his name would never be mentioned. This would also account for the fact that nothing incriminating was found in his possession.

(24) Q. What is his clerk's account of his attitude for two weeks previously (i.e. since hearing of the finding of the letter 'A'?).

A. He said Geary did no work during the period.

(25) Q. Did the clerk appear to be hostile to Geary?

A. No. On the contrary.

(26) Q. Did Supt. Geary make it his business to visit Supt. O'Driscoll in Dublin some months ago and question him on political matters in the city?

A. Yes. Report attached marked 'D' (not yet available).

(27) Q. Likely object of this?

A. Probably to give first hand information to the Irregulars, and it may be that he had a legitimate motive.

These are a few important points that I have endeavoured to cover.

Setting out with the firm conviction that the Supt. is guilty of this grave charge, it would be unnatural if bias against him did not creep in to fashion my thoughts and words, but I have as far as possible tried to fairly set out the facts of the case and draw reasonable deductions and inferences therefrom. The evidence against him is incomplete no doubt, as it must be in such cases, but it is sufficient, in my opinion, to be incontrovertible.

I have to strongly recommend that this man, whom I believe to have so betrayed his trust and besmirched the good name of the force, be dismissed with ignominy.

[The photocopy of the original carries the signature of David Neligan]

Chief Superintendent[2]

WILLIAM'S STATEMENT CONCERNING NELIGAN'S REPORT

William Geary wrote to his godson, Judge John P. Collins, on 11 February 1999; he commented incisively on David Neligan's long report of 20 June 1928, which Commissioner O'Duffy had attached to his report, 'Treachery, Supt. Geary, Kilrush', of the same date (quoted in full in Chapter 5 of this book).

Chief Superintendent David Neligan's report is long, very detailed, based on two intercepted letters from the IRA, in which my name is mentioned. He does not spare me. It may be divided into two parts, in one of which he gives his observations, the other of twenty-seven questions to himself and answers. His analysis of the items A and B sound plausible but when he starts his questions its weakness is disclosed. It is necessary to examine only a few having a bearing on the case.

Number 1. He says I was aware from the beginning that the IRA letters were examined by the police and considers it extraordinary since it was alleged that I was in league with them that I did not warn the IRA never to include my name in its communications. He admits he is baffled and has no answer.

Number 2. He thinks the IRA was not aware of letter censoring but qualifies that by saying they did not trust the post. My answer would be that every secret society takes into consideration that its letters are censored.

Number 6. He says I had securities and shares worth approximately £300, so I had, making me immune from greed.

Number 9. As to the possibility of a plot to ruin me, he thinks it is not worthy of consideration and too clever. He fails to suggest how simple it is to send letters through the mail, knowing they would be intercepted.

Numbers 10, 11, 12 and 13. These are related, raids were carried out, not too many I would say, to the dismay and discomfort of the IRA whose influence was on the wane, small dumps of arms were turned in (we knew in advance where they were) which would generate hostility against the police and to me.

Numbers 18, 19 and 20. I have no recollection.

Number 21. D.O. Keyes told me that I was to be offered a bribe

– my mistake that I did not consult the Chief Superintendent – but surely a guilty man would have done so – I did not take the matter seriously.

Number 25. Have no recollection of such a visit.

Finally, admitting that the evidence is incomplete, nevertheless, he has convinced himself of my guilt by reasonable deduction and recommends that I be dismissed with ignominy.

Commissioner Owen O'Duffy transmitted Chief Superintendent David Neligan's report to the Secretary, Minister for Justice, having accepted it completely. Naturally he was shocked with such a report as it really reflected unfavourably on him, there to be corruption in the Garda Síochána, on which he had made a large impact. He states that a criminal as I was alleged to be deserved capital punishment. He says he had strong suspicion of me, and goes on to say that I stood out alone of my remarkable knowledge of the Irregular organisation displayed at the recent conference of Superintendents from Clare, Limerick and Tipperary. Strangely I do not remember the meeting but if it was as he states I think I should be commended that a Garda Superintendent was cognisant of the subversive activity in his District.

He arranged to have me paraded before himself, Deputy Commissioner Éamonn Coogan and Chief Superintendent David Neligan to shock me by surprise in the hope that I would break down 'being regarded as a bit weak willed'. This took place in Carmody's Hotel, Ennis, County Clare, 16 June 1928. His report on confrontation is quite true and noted that I forcefully protested my innocence. He does not disclose that he said he had a receipt for a payment of £100 to me from the IRA nor does he mention that he offered me leniency for information from me.

He notes that after a thorough search of my room, bank books, personal belongings in Kilrush nothing incriminating was found, not even in the houses of Irregulars searched simultaneously. I was suspended from duty that evening.

I am amazed on reading my letter to the Adjutant, Depot, dated 19.6.1928 to which he refers. Before writing it, Superintendent Michael Higgins, my close friend, after seeing Neligan in the Depot that day, told me that Neligan told him that I was to be booted out of the Force. [It is significant that on 19 June 1928 David Neligan could confidently tell Superintendent Michael Higgins that William Geary would be 'booted out of the force'; this was before the decision of the Executive Council on 25 June 1928.] I was greatly upset at the news so I demanded legal assistance.

Commissioner O'Duffy, confident of my guilt and treachery, asserts that no useful purpose by an Inquiry, recommends that I be dismissed with ignominy forthwith, and in view of my letter of 19 the matter be dealt with immediately. The request reminds me of the appeal of Claudius, King of Denmark, to the English King that Hamlet's head be chopped off without waiting for grinding the axe.

Finally it was no great surprise to me that there was nothing in the file only two 'planted' letters, sufficient to delude the authorities taking no risk consistent with the political climate, at that time. It would not be very good policy to defend me fear rampant [*sic*].

There was a motive to destroy me, IRA frustration at the success of the Garda Síochána in gaining public confidence.

There is no doubt that Kilrush, Co. Clare and the surrounding area, of all places in Ireland, would be the most undesirable place for a Garda Superintendent to survive, still, I did not consider myself under any stress, found the people, except for a couple of churls, very nice and friendly, really I enjoyed working there, snipe shooting very good.

It must not be forgotten that the country had emerged from Civil War, and there was that young, untrained, inexperienced police force assigned to restore order.

Remarkable, that I alone, now within a few days of my hundredth birthday, the only survivor (a guess) of all the people mentioned in the file, and that the Lord has spared me to refute the baseless charge against me.

My thanks to those who believed my word and worked to clear my name,

William Geary[3]

WILLIAM'S LETTER REGARDING THE DEPARTMENT OF JUSTICE FILE RELEASED BY JOHN O'DONOGHUE, TD, MINISTER FOR JUSTICE

On 3 February 1999 William received the excerpts (some of it redacted) from the Department of Justice file released by John O'Donoghue, TD, Minister for Justice. Below is the letter he wrote on 11 February 1999 to his godson Judge John P. Collins:

Dear John:

I have copied the file for me to keep, you to have the original which you deserve.

You may assume that I have studied the file carefully since you gave it to me on 3 February 1999 and I hope you approve of my report on it.

Since I wrote the report I had another idea which I should have included but hated to do it again. In the letter marked 'A', of 12 June 1928, to the C.O. West Clare Bn. there is mention of 'stuff' and 'documents'. I wish someone would enlighten me on what is meant, as I know of none, unless is meant the names of informers only known to the detectives, there being no paid informers. The letter is mere fiction, had to be to make the item marked 'B' to scan authentic – a back-up.

When you read the file, I think you shall agree it is no wonder that it was kept under wraps all those years, the so-called evidence was spurious.

Best wishes

Willie.[4]

WILLIAM'S STATEMENT CONCERNING VINDICATION

There is on file in the Garda Museum, Dublin Castle, a copy of a letter dated 12 May 1999 from John P. Collins advising that there is a statement attached from William Geary shortly after he heard the 'news'. Consider for a moment the emotions of a 100-year-old man as his trembling hands opened the packet, as his eyes fell on the contents, how his heart raced, how his joy surged to find that no evidence existed to condemn him. Below is his statement:

TO WHOM IT MAY CONCERN
A STATEMENT OF WILLIAM GEARY
SUPERINTENDENT GARDA SÍOCHÁNA (RET)

1   At this hour of triumph I have to be wary, not to be carried away, or gloat.

2   I cannot understand why God has singled me out for such an eventful life, given me excellent health, even now at 100 years of age, and while I have been humbled He has given me so much to be grateful for.

3   On 16 June 1928 in Carmody's Hotel in Ennis, County Clare, I was told by Garda Commissioner Eoin O'Duffy, in the presence of Deputy Commissioner Éamonn Coogan, Chief Superintendent David Neligan and Edward O'Duffy, Chief Superintendent County Clare, he had solid evidence (a receipt) I took a bribe of £100.0.0 from the Republicans for information. The charge was absolutely false, and I protested my innocence. I was the Superintendent of the Garda Síochána, Kilrush, County Clare at the time. That same day in a thorough examination of my books in Kilrush, my bank account, and lodgings nothing was found to incriminate me. I was suspended from duty that evening, dismissed from the Force, 25 June 1928, by the Executive Council, Irish Free State, without an enquiry or anything else.

4   I emigrated to the United States, November 1928, branded

a traitor, humiliated before the world, a stigma I have had to bear for over 70 years, until now.

5   The few simple facts of my dismissal from the Garda Síochána are so strange it is a wonder anyone would believe me, so it was not surprising that I was told by many people I should forget it, visit Ireland, as no one remembered. I was ashamed I could not do that.

6   This statement is to pay tribute and thanks to a few people who applied their energy on my behalf. Over a period of 70 years I cannot remember every name, but I hope you understand that each and every one has my prayerful thanks.

7   In 1932, Mr Donagh O'Brien, TD, Limerick put my case before Mr P. J. Rutledge, TD, Minister for Justice. Mr Rutledge wrote that there was strong evidence against me, that I had to produce new evidence and that he, O'Brien, had better not bother himself about me. Next, the Reverend Donald O'Callaghan, Carmelite; John Vincent Moran, reporter, *Limerick Leader*, the first newspaper to give me media publicity; Mr Frank Prendergast, TD, Limerick Lab., who brought the matter before the Dáil; my godson Judge John Patrick Collins, Justice of the Supreme Court of the State of New York, over a period of years requested the file under the Freedom of Information Act, but to no avail; Mr Tim Leahy, author of *Memoirs of a Garda Superintendent*, instrumental in bringing my case to the attention of Mr Conor Brady, Editor, *Irish Times*; Miss Margaret Ward, reporter, *Irish Times*; Reverend Thomas Carroll, Longford. At one time in the seventies, after a certain Minister for Justice wrote to inform me that as all

the papers of my case were 'pulped' then no Government could act merely on my statements, my plea for justice looked extremely bleak. (I may add here thanks to Mr Prendergast, TD, it became known that the file did actually exist.)

8   All of a sudden things changed when Miss Ward's full page article was published in *The Irish Times*, which induced the Government to release the partial file to me, 3 February 1999.

9   Before opening the envelope, I wondered what possibly could be there to justify my dismissal from the Garda Síochána since I had taken no bribe. To my surprise there were only decoded intercepted despatches between the West Clare Battalion, IRA, and its Headquarters to indicate that I had accepted a bribe of £100.0.0 for information. The despatches, apparently, were substituted by Mr Seán MacBride, Chief of Staff to delude the Garda Síochána, and answered to the request of the West Clare Battalion for permission to do violence to me. Strange as it may seem, I had no apprehension of any danger to me in 1928.

10 I admire the present Irish Government who had the courage to set aside previous adverse decisions, render justice to me long delayed, in particular my good name. In this regard, I want to thank Mr Bertie Ahern, TD, Taoiseach, and Mr John O'Donoghue, TD, Minister for Justice for their initiative, whose names shall go down in history.

Despite what happened to me there, I still have a deep affection for the people of West Clare, where I spent two happy years, in Kilrush.

Finally I take this opportunity to thank each and every one who called to congratulate me on my rehabilitation.

Sincerely

William Geary

Bayside, N.Y.

25 April 1999[5]

Appendix 3:
The Coded Message

When William opened the file copies from the Department of Justice, Equality and Law Reform on 3 February 1999 he could read the following on page one of David Neligan's report of 20 June 1928: 'For the last two years Scotland Yard has helped us in the decoding of cipher messages. As certain of these letters contained such messages which defied our expert I asked Col. Carter to help, and he consented.' The allegations against William Geary relied solely on the decoding of the IRA document. The file did not include an image of the original letter, so anyone reading it had to rely on the unauthenticated wording received from Scotland Yard.

In the second of Margaret Ward's reports in *The Irish Times* of 27 February 1999, Ward wrote:

Only a few of the old documents indicate the basis for Mr Geary's removal. The main evidence against him is in two intercepted IRA letters with encoded message … The second, a badly photocopied document, or photo, is completely illegible except for a decoded message reading:

'Have handed over the hundred pounds to Superintendent

Geary. He was very satisfied with the amount. I have given him list of houses which can be safely raided from time to time. It would be well to hit up Geary as hard as possible in An Phoelacht (sic) as he is working satisfactory. Let me know if I may drop the other C.I.D. Have sent on by courier the latest stuff as it is important you should have it at once.'[6]

William Geary had to accept the message at face value because it was impossible to decode the smudged photocopy that accompanied it. On 12 November 2009 I was afforded access to the Geary files in the Department of Justice; there I was astounded to discover the original photograph of the intercepted message. Fortunately I was aware of the publication *Decoding the IRA* by Tom Mahon and James Gillogly. Dr Tom Mahon graduated from University College Dublin as a medical doctor in 1983; he is a consultant radiologist and also an accomplished historian who has researched the IRA for over ten years. Professor James (Jim) Gillogly specialises in cryptanalysis and has solved several of the world's most famous unsolved codes. I was afforded the utmost help and encouragement from these gentlemen. Gillogly told me:[7]

The Geary message was sent in the same type of columnar transposition cipher as most of our IRA traffic, using the key DISTINGUISHED. DISTINGUISHED is indeed the key we found for West Clare Battn in message P69/193(34).

He provided the following decryption:

have handed over the hundrep pounds to supt geary he was very satisfied with the amount i have given him list of houses which can be safely raided from time to time it would be well to hit up geary as hard as possible in an phoblacht as he is working satisfactory let me know if i may drop the other cid haue sent on by courier the latest stuff as it is important you should have it at once

He explained further:

I've left the typos (hundrep->hundred, haue->have), as they don't interfere with the sense. I have added word divisions, which are not given in the cipher itself. Hope this helps – I'd be interested to hear your conclusions. Let me know if you need to see the details of the encryption for further evidence.

Fortified with this information I am now confident that we are dealing with an IRA message which uses the code associated with West Clare where Superintendent William Geary was stationed in Kilrush. Neligan's handwritten letter to William, dated 11 June 1971, identifies the source as being T. J. Ryan, Kilrush, who was the IRA commander in West Clare. The IRA message had more than seventy handwritten words and hundreds of characters; with the aid of a handwriting expert this could have been compared with T. J. Ryan's hand to provide vital evidence against the IRA.

For the reader's benefit I requested that Professor Gillogly break down the deciphering process. In the final chart below I have shown 'SUPTGEARY' in bold. It is my theory that this was a ploy to incriminate Superintendent Geary and should have been dismissed as spurious because the IRA would not divulge the name of a valuable source; my assumption is supported by Tom Mahon, who writes in the introduction of *Decoding the IRA*: 'For security purposes the IRA were deliberately indirect and cryptic. Even in cipher. For instance, only rarely were the IRA leaders or key agents referred to by their real names; instead they were assigned a pseudonym or referred to by rank.'[8]

Gillogly, however, takes an opposing point of view, indicating that there were hundreds of incidences in which persons were named, for example, 'we have information that sean hogan has offered his services to nelligan for money he may therefore be used in tipp' and (one including a title) 'guard mp wall clerk in supt mcmahons office at guard depot in Dublin I am told he is acquainted with miss lil coventry'.

I have examined many records, assertions, hypotheses, speculations and conjectures and I remain convinced that the message was designed to deceive the Irish police, who fell into a trap so often employed by the IRA previously.

Below is Professor Gillogly's first message regarding the decryption.

GEARY DECRYPTION, FIRST MESSAGE BY JIM GILLOGLY, 17 DECEMBER 2009

1. Write the 13-letter keyword.

D   I   S   T   I   N   G   U   I   S   H   E   D

2. Draw a frame under it large enough for the whole message, in this case twenty-four full lines.

If the last line is not full, truncate it by the right amount.

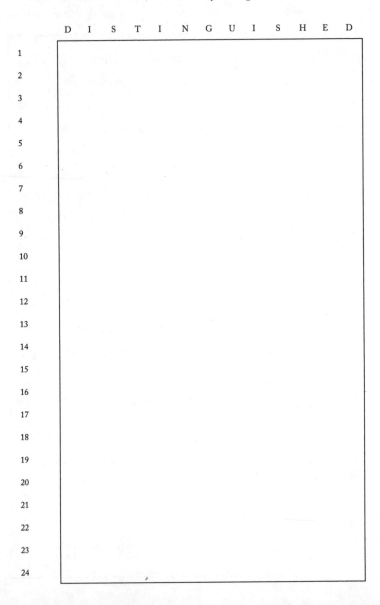

3. Write the first two rows of the cipher into the frame by columns, alphabetically by key letters.

If two or more key letters are the same, use the left-most first.

	D	I	S	T	I	N	G	U	I	S	H	E	D
1	H											V	E
2	R											P	O
3	U											E	A
4	R											S	A
5	T											T	H
6	E											E	G
7	I											O	F
8	H												A
9	N												D
10	E												T
11	I												W
12	E												A
13	R												S
14	S												O
15	B												W
16	O												A
17	C												O
18	W												H
19	E												E
20	S												I
21	E												T
22	U												O
23	R												L
24	D												E

4. Continue writing the rows in, double-checking your entry by seeing whether words start forming.

Here are the next two rows.

	D	I	S	T	I	N	G	U	I	S	H	E	D
1	H						N				O	V	E
2	R						N				P	P	O
3	U						S				G	E	A
4	R						S				Y	S	A
5	T						D				H	T	H
6	E						T				V	E	G
7	I						H				T	O	F
8	H						W				H	C	A
9	N						E				A	I	D
10	E						T				T	O	T
11	I						O				B	O	W
12	E						I				G	E	A
13	R						R				P	O	S
14	S						I				P	H	O
15	B						A				I	S	W
16	O						S				S	F	A
17	C						E				K	N	O
18	W						Y				P	T	H
19	E						C				A	U	E
20	S						B					R	I
21	E						A					S	T
22	U						T					P	O
23	R						O					U	L
24	D						T					C	E

5. Note that we're already seeing words forming: OVER, GEAR (twice),
THE, KNOW.

Continue until all the cipher text has been entered in the frame.

	D	I	S	T	I	N	G	U	I	S	H	E	D
1	H	A	V	E	H	A	N	D	E	D	O	V	E
2	R	T	H	E	H	U	N	D	R	E	P	P	O
3	U	N	D	S	T	O	S	U	P	T	G	E	A
4	R	Y	H	E	W	A	S	V	E	R	Y	S	A
5	T	I	S	F	I	E	D	W	I	T	H	T	H
6	E	A	M	O	U	N	T	I	H	A	V	E	G
7	I	V	E	N	H	I	M	L	I	S	T	O	F
8	H	O	U	S	E	S	W	H	I	C	H	C	A
9	N	B	E	S	A	F	E	L	Y	R	A	I	D
10	E	D	F	R	O	M	T	I	M	E	T	O	T
11	I	M	E	I	T	W	O	U	L	D	B	E	W
12	E	L	L	T	O	H	I	T	U	P	G	E	A
13	R	Y	A	S	H	A	R	D	A	S	P	O	S
14	S	S	I	B	L	E	I	N	A	N	P	H	O
15	B	L	A	C	H	T	A	S	H	E	I	S	W
16	O	R	K	I	N	G	S	A	T	I	S	F	A
17	C	T	O	R	Y	L	E	T	M	E	K	N	O
18	W	I	F	I	M	A	Y	D	R	O	P	T	H
19	E	O	T	H	E	R	C	I	D	H	A	U	E
20	S	E	N	T	O	N	B	Y	C	O	U	R	I
21	E	R	T	H	E	L	A	T	E	S	T	S	T
22	U	F	F	A	S	I	T	I	S	I	M	P	O
23	R	T	A	N	T	Y	O	U	S	H	O	U	L
24	D	H	A	V	E	I	T	A	T	O	N	C	E

6. There are two errors (using my transcription) in the above, both of which appear also in your transcription: HUNDREP and HAUE.

The P in HUNDREP comes from the H column, which is filled starting at OPGY HVTHA, in the middle of line 4 of the cipher.

The offending 'D' is the P of the group TOPGY. It's likely that when copying it from the worksheet the encryptor didn't read the letter correctly.

The U in HAUE comes from the E column, which is filled starting at VP ESTEO at the end of the second line of the cipher.

The incorrect 'U' is in the TURSP, the third group of the third row. This one you and I both read as a U, but could just as easily be read as a V.

In neither case are we confused about the actual meaning.

Appendix 4:
Criminal Activity of
S-Branch Officers

Revelations about the criminal activity of S-Branch officers ultimately brought about the dismissal of David Neligan. Below is File Jus/8/376, 'Copy of findings of sworn enquiry held at Kilrush on the 7th, 8th, 9th, & 10th of September 1932', which contains such revelations:

N.A. 'File Jus/8/376'
Copy of findings of sworn enquiry held at Kilrush on the 7th, 8th, 9th, & 10th of September 1932.

From the evidence before us we find:

(1) That Detective Officers Myles Muldowney and Michael Christopher Carroll and members of the party consisting of George Gilmore and others were guilty of jeering at and taunting each other at Cappa Road, Kilrush on the night of Sunday, 14th August 1932 but that Messrs Gilmore, Ryan and Lowe did not take part therein.

(2) That Detective Officers Myles Muldowney and Michael Christopher Carroll followed the party consisting of George

Gilmore and others for a distance not warranted by the duty on which they were engaged and that without justification they fired at and wounded Messrs Gilmore and Ryan.

(3) That no shots were fired by the party consisting of Messrs Gilmore, Ryan and others.

(4) That the said Detective Officers Muldowney and Carroll caused Messrs Gilmore, Ryan and Lowe to be wrongfully charged with shooting at and attempting to murder them, the said detective officers, and, for the purpose of causing them to be charged deceived their own Superior Officers by making to them false and misleading statements. We are of opinion that the Superior Officers acted in good faith having been misled by these false statements.

(5) That in the effect of arresting T. J. Ryan at Kilrush Hospital, Detective Officer Myles Muldowney and Matthew Mulkeen committed a serious assault on the said T. J. Ryan by beating him about the head with their revolvers, but that having regard to our find at No. 4 above, although Detective Officer Muldowney knew that the arrest was unjustified, Detective Officer Mulkeen was not so aware.

(6) We are of opinion that the complaints of delay in conveying T. J. Ryan to Hospital after arrest have not been established and that Superintendent Feeney and Sergeant Reilly did everything in their power to have him removed to Hospital as soon as possible after his arrival at the Garda Station. We find that during his detention in the Station he was not in any way ill-treated.

(7) Regarding the allegation of the ill-treatment of Mr George

Gilmore in the Hospital we are of opinion that he was unnecessarily disturbed and annoyed, having regard to his condition, by Detective Officer Thomas Murphy but that the charge in this respect against officers Bernard Hanley and James Brennan has not been proven. No allegation was made against Detective Officers Patrick McCaffrey and James Hughes and we are satisfied that they acted with every consideration.

(8) That the allegations regarding the ill-treatment of Mr T. J. Ryan in Hospital have not been sustained.

Dated 15 day of September 1932.

Signed: Patrick Lynch (K.C.)

John McGrath (Solicitor)

Daniel J. Browne (Solicitor)[9]

Endnotes

INTRODUCTION

1 Private collection.

2 Shakespeare, W., *Othello*, act 3, scene 3.

CHAPTER 1

1 Neligan's report is discussed in detail in Chapter 5 and reproduced in full in Appendix 2. William's analysis of it in a letter to Judge John P. Collins is also reproduced in Appendix 2.

CHAPTER 2

1 First Class Certificate of Proficiency no. 8255.

2 'Article 1', Constitution of the Irish Free State (Saorstát Éireann), Act No. 1 of 1922.

3 Geary files, Garda Museum, Dublin Castle.

CHAPTER 3

1 Ryan, M., *Liam Lynch – The Real Chief* (Mercier Press, Cork and Dublin, 1986), pp. 146–7; in the War of Independence the British had resorted to terrorism and the shooting of IRA prisoners. The IRA's response was to order the shooting of captured officers, while captured soldiers and police were released since they could not be imprisoned. Ernie O'Malley describes the dramatic capture and execution of three gunnery officers from Fethard Barracks in 1920, despite his own misgivings: 'If we are surrounded,' O'Malley said to the officers, 'I'll let you go. I'm not going to shoot you like dogs.' The combat-hardened O'Malley remarked, 'It seemed easier to face one's own execution than to shoot others.' – O'Malley, E., *Army Without Banners: Adventures of an Irish Volunteer* (Houghton Mifflin

Company, Boston, 1937), pp. 392–8.

2 Macardle, D., *Tragedies of Kerry 1922–1923*, 10th ed. (Irish Book Bureau, Dublin, 1924), p. 15.

3 Dáil Éireann. Questions – Kerry prisoners deaths, Vols 3–17 April 1923 (National Archives, Bishop Street, Dublin). The inquiry members were Major General P. O'Daly, Major General Éamonn Price and Colonel J. McGuinness.

4 'Executive Council Minutes' (cabinet), G 2/3, 13 December 1923, p. 87.

5 G 2/3, 22 January 1924, p. 136, (National Archives, Bishop Street, Dublin); these cabinet notes were signed into the record by the authority of William T. Cosgrave.

6 Dáil Éireann. Questions. Oral Answers – Treatment of Clare Prisoners, Vol. 29, 24 April 1929 (National Archives, Bishop Street, Dublin); Lynch, P., McGrath, J. and Browne, D. J. 'File Jus/8/376: copy of findings of sworn enquiry held at Kilrush on 7, 8, 9 and 10 September 1932' (National Archives, Bishop Street, Dublin), 15 September 1932 (signed Patrick Lynch KC, John McGrath (solicitor) and Daniel J. Browne (solicitor).

7 Sinn Féin (literally 'we ourselves') was a political party founded by Arthur Griffith on 28 November 1905; the policy was to establish in Ireland's capital a national legislature endowed with the moral authority of the Irish nation.

8 O'Duffy, E., *General Order 1922*, Garda Museum, Dublin Castle, 21 November 1922.

9 Commissioner Eoin O'Duffy was a pompous egoist. After becoming commissioner he began to use the Irish version of his name; the former Owen O'Duffy became Eoin Ua Dubhthaigh. Throughout his life he was entitled to the honour of General. The word '*Taoiseach*' means leader, a title never used by any other commissioner. '*Coimisinéir*' is the Irish word for commissioner.

10 McGarry, F., *Eoin O'Duffy: A Self-Made Hero* (Oxford University Press, Oxford, 2005), p. 92.

11 The political party named Fianna Fáil had its origins in Sinn Féin.

12 McGarry (2005), p. 92.

13 National Archives, Bishop Street, Dublin.

CHAPTER 4

1 His garda registration number was 938.

2 Dáil Éireann. Debate – The Garda Síochána (Temporary Provisions) Act, No. 37 of 1923, 8 August 1923 (National Archives, Bishop Street, Dublin).

3 The test was established on 14 April 1924.

4 Gallagher, J., Diary, Private collection.

5 'Executive Council Minutes' (cabinet), G 2/3, Concerning crime in Saorstát Éireann, (National Archives, Bishop Street, Dublin), 26 February 1924, p. 168.

6 McGarry (2005), p. 80.

7 Dowling's garda registration number was 5708.

8 Fennelly, T., *Fitz* (Arderin Publishing Company in conjunction with the Leinster Express, Kildare, 1997); see Chapter 10 'The Civil War'. Fitz was Colonel Fitzmaurice, who flew in a Junkers W33 aircraft, *Bremen*, on the first east–west transatlantic flight, from Baldonnell on 12 April 1928.

9 Neligan, D., 'Irregular Papers Implicating Superintendent Geary', From Chief Superintendent Neligan to Commissioner Eoin O'Duffy, Department of the Taoiseach, Ref. CS 270/28, 20 June 1928, Geary files, Garda Museum, Dublin Castle.

10 Such a 'poppy' is an artificial corn poppy, made of plastic and cardboard by disabled ex-servicemen, worn in the United Kingdom and other Commonwealth countries from late October to Remembrance Sunday in November in support of the Royal British Legion's Poppy Appeal and to remember those servicemen and women who died in war.

11 Within a year of William's departure from Kilrush, activity by the IRA increased. In one incident Detective Officer T. O'Sullivan of Knock sub-district was killed. On 11 June 1929 Detective Officer O'Driscoll received an anonymous letter stating: 'I found a box of ammunition and papers in a butt of hay in the haggard. The times are dangerous, I was afraid to keep it near the place: I threw it inside the ditch at Lahiff Cross in Ardill's meadow yesterday. I want you to take it away; I do not want to get into trouble with people around here (Signed) Farmer.' (quoted in Coogan, T. P., *The IRA* (London, Palgrave Macmillan, 2002)).

O'Driscoll found the box, and carried it to Tullycrine; there he met O'Sullivan and another garda. While they were trying to open the box it blew up and the explosion killed O'Sullivan outright. At Tullycrine a temporary post was located to shelter gardaí giving protection to a landowner threatened in a land war.

12 *Garda Review*, February 1927, p. 149.

13 Geary files, Garda Museum, Dublin Castle.

14 Newspaper archives, Local Studies, Clare County Library.

CHAPTER 5

1 The garda division of Clare comprised five districts (Ennis, Ennistymon, Ballyvaughan, Kilrush and Killaloe). Chief Superintendent O'Duffy was in charge of Clare division; Superintendent Geary was in charge of Kilrush district.

2 Geary, W., Sworn affidavit made before a Notary Public in New York, accompanying a letter from a Carmelite Priest to Taoiseach Jack Lynch, Geary file, Department of Justice, 8 January 1968.

3 He retained the deputy commissioner post until 1936, when he was removed from office after an altercation with the general manager of *The Irish Press* in the Gresham Hotel, Dublin. He was reappointed chief superintendent in charge of traffic and retired on 1 August 1941, after which he qualified as a barrister. He entered politics and was elected as a Fine Gael Deputy for Carlow/Kilkenny in 1944; he sought re-election in 1948 but died on 2 January after a short illness. During his tenure as deputy commissioner, he took command of the gardaí and as inspector general of the defence forces, when Commissioner O'Duffy was away for protracted periods in America.

4 'Executive Council Minutes' (cabinet), (National Archives, Bishop Street, Dublin).

5 He continued in the garda service until 1932, when he was dismissed for organising a collection for dismissed Special Branch men convicted of shooting IRA men and relegated to an obscure post in the Land Commission by Taoiseach Eamon de Valera.

6 Geary, W., Affidavit, Geary files, Garda Museum, Dublin Castle, 8 January 1968.

7   O'Duffy, E., 'Alleged Treachery – Supt. Geary, Kilrush', Report to the
     Secretary of the Department of Justice, Office of the Taoiseach, 20 June
     1928.

8   *Ibid.*

9   The renowned cryptographer Professor James (Jim) Gillogly, who
     decoded the copy of the message, said: 'The Geary message was sent
     in the same type of columnar transposition cipher as most of our
     IRA traffic, using the key DISTINGUISHED. DISTINGUISHED
     is indeed the key we found for West Clare Battalion in message
     P69/193(34) … I've left the typos (hundrep->hundred, haue->have), as
     they don't interfere with the sense. I have added word divisions, which
     are not given in the cipher itself …'; see also Mahon, T. and Gillogly, J.
     Decoding the IRA (Mercier Press, Cork, 2008).

10   Geary, W., 'Re engaging of a Solicitor – Supt. W. Geary. R.O. C.241,
     August 1927', Statement to Commandant Stack, Geary files, Garda
     Museum, Dublin Castle, 19 June 1928.

11   The Routine Order quoted by Geary expressed his civil rights, but more
     important are his rights under the internal Garda Regulations: p. 70 of
     Routine Orders, August 1927 states: '241 When members of the Force,
     who are charged with an offence against discipline, desire to employ a
     Solicitor to aid them in their defence before an Enquiry they should
     obtain the Commissioner's permission beforehand.'

12   Geary, W., Affidavit, Geary file, Department of Justice, 20 January
     1992.

13   Neligan (20 June 1928).

14   On 18 December 2009 I was informed by Professor James Gillogly,
     co-author of *Decoding the IRA*, that this code 'had certainly been in use
     for at least two years at that point'.

15   O'Duffy (20 June 1928).

16   Section 7 reads: 'Subject to the provisions of paragraphs 22 to 25
     (inclusive) of these regulations, every member of the Force against
     whom a disciplinary charge is being preferred shall (unless the charge
     involves a criminal offence which is or will be the subject of proceedings
     before the Courts) be informed in writing, as soon as possible of the
     nature of the charge preferred against him. The written charge shall

be set out on a form provided for that purpose (hereinafter referred to as the Misconduct Form) and shall disclose the offence or offences alleged, with such particulars of time and place as will leave the accused under no misapprehension as to the offence with which he is charged. The accused shall be directed to state in writing upon the Misconduct Form whether he admits or denies the charge. Such admission or denial must not be qualified in any way, but the accused may be allowed to attach any explanation which he may wish to offer in writing. An offence against discipline will be aggravated by a denial of the charge.'

17 Coakley's garda registration number was 1574.

18 O'Duffy, E., Letter to the Department of Justice, Department of Justice, 9 November 1928.

19 O'Duffy also drew adverse conclusions about the 'influence of Miss Barrett with whom he [Coakley] kept company', seemingly not considering the possibility that as a detective he may have been seeking information about the activities of the IRA. He also reported that 'Coakley was a coward', not acknowledging the facts that Coakley (1) helped establish Ennistymon barracks on 13 October 1922 during the Civil War; (2) Arrested an armed robber in 1923; and (3) Served in North Clare during the period when Garda Dowling was murdered.

20 Gallagher, J., Diary, Private collection; the diary entries are from 1 November 1925 to 1 August 1928.

21 'Executive Council Minutes' (cabinet), G 2/7, 'Garda Síochána – Dismissal of Sup't William Geary. An order was made dismissing Superintendent William Geary from the Garda Síochána with effect as from 25 June 1928' (National Archives, Bishop Street, Dublin), 25 June 1928, p. 106.

22 Garda Síochána. (Discipline) Regulations, Section 1. (2) (b), & (5) (a), & (8) (d), & (27) (Government Publications, Molesworth Street, Dublin 2, 1926): 'tyrannical conduct' – 'knowingly makes or signs any false, misleading or inaccurate statement return or certificate ... exceeds his duty in any manner to the prejudice of good order and discipline; by concealment, or wilful omission or otherwise, attempting to evade the true spirit and meaning of the orders and regulations governing the Force.'

CHAPTER 6

1   Six gardaí were killed in the period 1922 to 1926.

2   Geary files, Garda Museum, Dublin Castle.

3   *Ibid.*

4   File S/34/28 of 16/4/1934, Geary file, Department of the Taoiseach, 16 April 1934.

5   William liked to recall that in 1922 when he was in Ballybay, County Monaghan, a woman had read his cards just for fun; she had said, 'You are going to wear another uniform.' Her prophecy came true twenty years later when he wore the uniform of the United States army. Coincidentally, the last three digits of his army number were 938 – identical to his registered number in Garda Síochána, file 237/162, 15 July 1950.

6   Geary files, Garda Museum, Dublin Castle.

7   This was an informal note between the Department of Justice and the Commissioner; it was initialled, not signed; Department of Justice.

8   File B.1/4327/28, (Confidential) 'Letter from the Assistant Commissioner to The Secretary, Department of Justice', Department of Justice, no date.

9   File B.1/4327/28, (Confidential) Margin note (1 August 1950) to 'Letter from the Assistant Commissioner to The Secretary, Department of Justice', Department of Justice, no date.

CHAPTER 7

1   Geary files, Garda Museum, Dublin Castle.

2   Section 24, Garda Síochána (Discipline) Regulations 1926 (Government Publications, Molesworth Street, Dublin 2).

3   Neligan, D., *The Spy in the Castle* (Gill & Macmillan, Dublin, 1968).

4   Geary files, Garda Museum, Dublin Castle.

5   Neligan, D., Statement to the Department of Justice, Geary file, Department of the Taoiseach, 14 October 1972.

6   Geary file, Department of Justice.

7   *Ibid.*

8   Geary files, Garda Museum, Dublin Castle.

9   *Ibid.*

10 *Ibid.*

11 Geary file, Department of Justice.

12 *Ibid.*

13 *Ibid.*

14 *Ibid.*

15 *Ibid.*

16 Geary file, Department of Justice; Geary files, Garda Museum, Dublin Castle.

17 Geary, W., Sworn affidavit made before Inez Simmons, Notary Public, State of New York, Geary files, Garda Museum, Dublin Castle, 29 July 1986.

18 Valerie Kelly, research officer of the Labour Party, Leinster House, Dublin.

19 Geary files, Garda Museum, Dublin Castle.

CHAPTER 8

1 National Archives, Bishop Street, Dublin.

2 Geary files, Garda Museum, Dublin Castle.

3 *Ibid.*

4 Geary file, Department of the Taoiseach.

5 Father Carroll (1933–2005) came from a family of four boys (James, Thomas, Anthony and Gerard) and one girl (Helen). All the boys pursued academic careers and became Catholic priests. Fr Thomas, a priest of the diocese of Ardagh and Clonmacnoise, spent most of his career abroad, studying in Rome, and teaching at the universities of Dallas and Notre Dame in North America.

6 The government was an uneasy alliance between Fianna Fáil and Labour; the Taoiseach, Charles Haughey, resigned when a former Minister for Justice, Sean Doherty, revealed that he had authorised illegal phone tapping. Albert Reynolds, TD, became Taoiseach and a controversy arose because his appointee, Harry Whelahan, was in office as Attorney General when there was undue delay in extraditing a priest to Northern Ireland on charges of child sexual abuse. This led to a series of allegations after Taoiseach Albert Reynolds appointed Harry Whelehan to the post of President of the High Court. The

government collapsed shortly after this; William Geary's travails paled into insignificance.

7   The Freedom of Information Act 1997 came into force on 21 April 1998 for government departments and offices and certain other government bodies, and on 21 October 1998 for local authorities and health boards. On 17 September 1998 (File Ref FOI 1998/0046) Miriam Dollard in the Taoiseach's Office (referring to file S 9051) suggested that some assistance might be available at Garda Síochána headquarters or in the Department of Justice, Equality and Law Reform. She wrote again on 23 September saying, 'I am examining these papers at present and I will be in touch with you again as soon as possible.'

8   Leahy, T., *Memoirs of a Garda Superintendent* (Hero Press, Kilrush, 1996).

9   *The Irish Times*, 20 February 1998; it should be noted that Conor Brady's rapport with Tim Leahy was partially due to the fact that his father, Cornelius Brady, had also been a superintendent in the Garda Síochána and had served in Clare.

10 Private collection.

11 *Ibid.*

12 *Ibid.*

13 *Ibid.*

14 *Ibid.*

15 Ward, M., 'Seventy years trying to clear his name', *The Irish Times*, 23 January 1999, p. 8.

16 Walsh, D., 'Superintendent's dismissal clearly invalid', *The Irish Times*, 23 January 1999.

17 'Soon after he requested a solicitor he was sacked without any charges, a hearing or a trial', *The Irish Times*, 27 February 1999.

18 Ward, M., 'Former garda says he was unfairly sacked in 1928 on the IRA's word', *The Irish Times*, 27 February 1999.

19 Private collection.

20 *Ibid.*

21 Paraphrased version of Brady, C. 'Leading article', *The Irish Times*, 13 April 1999.

22 Geary file, Department of Justice; Geary files, Garda Museum, Dublin Castle.

23 Private collection.

24 Geary, W., 'To Whom it May Concern: A Statement of William Geary Superintendent Garda Síochána (Ret)', Geary files, Garda Museum, Dublin Castle, 25 April 1999.

AFTERWORD

1 Private collection.

2 'Leading article: Fair Play at Last', *The Irish Times*, 23 April 1999; emphasis added.

3 Mr O'Donoghue was in Manhattan at the invitation of the John Jay College of Criminal Justice and the donation honoured the memory of Garda Jerry McCabe, who was killed by the IRA in Adare, County Limerick, in June 1996.

4 A story by Tom Brady in the *Irish Independent* told of the upcoming meeting; *The Irish Times* reported on the meeting: Ward, M. 'Linked hands recall Geary's fight for justice', *The Irish Times*, 17 November 1999, p. 11.

5 Ward, M., 'Linked hands recall Geary's fight for justice', *The Irish Times*, 17 November 1999, p. 11.

6 Geary, W., 'Letter', *IPA Journal*, February 2003, p. 73.

7 *The Irish Times*, 23 October 2004.

8 Colvert, B. K., Colgan, K., 'Appreciations: William Geary: 28th February 1899–14th October 2004', *IPA Journal*, December 2004, pp. 130–1.

APPENDICES

1 Geary, W., 'Re engaging of a Solicitor – Supt. W. Geary. R.O. C.241, August 1927', Statement to Commandant Stack, Geary files, Garda Museum, Dublin Castle, 19 June 1928; originally this document was written by hand. Geary requested return of his handwritten report and was advised that it did not exist. The copy was typed.

2 Neligan (20 June 1928).

3 Private collection (to be lodged in the Garda Museum, Dublin Castle).

4   *Ibid.*

5   Geary, W., 'To Whom it May Concern: A Statement of William Geary Superintendent Garda Síochána (Ret)', Geary files, Garda Museum, Dublin Castle, 25 April 1999.

6   Ward, M., 'Former garda says he was unfairly sacked in 1928 on the IRA's word', *The Irish Times*, 27 February 1999.

7   See Chapter 5, endnote 9.

8   Mahon, T. and Gillogly, J., *Decoding the IRA* (Mercier Press, Cork, 2008), p. 14.

9   Lynch, P., McGrath, J. and Browne, D. J., 'File Jus/8/376: copy of findings of sworn enquiry held at Kilrush on 7, 8, 9 and 10 September 1932' (National Archives, Bishop Street, Dublin), 15 September 1932.

BIBLIOGRAPHY

PRIMARY SOURCES

An Garda Síochána, Routine Orders (R.O. C.241 of August 1927)

Dáil Éireann, Debate – The Garda Síochána (Temporary Provisions) Act, No. 37 of 1923, 8 August 1923 (National Archives, Bishop Street, Dublin)

Dáil Éireann, Questions – Kerry prisoners deaths, Vols 3–17 April 1923 (National Archives, Bishop Street, Dublin)

Dáil Éireann, Questions – Oral Answers – Treatment of Clare Prisoners, Vol. 29, 24 April 1929 (National Archives, Bishop Street, Dublin)

'Executive Council Minutes' (cabinet), G 2/3, (National Archives, Bishop Street, Dublin), 13 December 1923

'Executive Council Minutes' (cabinet), G 2/3, (National Archives, Bishop Street, Dublin), 22 January 1924

'Executive Council Minutes' (cabinet), G 2/3, Concerning crime in Saorstát Éireann, (National Archives, Bishop Street, Dublin), 26 February 1924

'Executive Council Minutes' (cabinet), G 2/7, 'Garda Síochána – Dismissal of Sup't William Geary. An order was made dismissing Superintendent William Geary from the Garda Síochána with effect as from 25 June 1928' (National Archives, Bishop Street, Dublin), 25 June 1928

Gallagher, J., Diary, Private collection

Geary file, Department of An Taoiseach

Geary file, Department of Justice

Geary files, Garda Museum, Dublin Castle

Geary, W., Affidavit, Geary file, Department of Justice, 20 January 1992

Geary, W., 'Re engaging of a Solicitor – Supt. W. Geary. R.O. C.241, August 1927', Statement to Commandant Stack, Geary files, Garda Museum, Dublin Castle, 19 June 1928

Geary, W., Sworn affidavit made before a Notary Public in New York, accompanying a letter from a Carmelite Priest to Taoiseach Jack Lynch, Geary file, Department of Justice, 8 January 1968

Geary, W., Sworn affidavit made before Inez Simmons, Notary Public, State of New York, Geary files, Garda Museum, Dublin Castle, 29 July 1986

Geary, W., 'To Whom it May Concern: A Statement of William Geary Superintendent Garda Síochána (Ret)', Geary files, Garda Museum, Dublin Castle, 25 April 1999

Lynch, P., McGrath, J. & Browne, D. J., 'File Jus/8/376: copy of findings of sworn enquiry held at Kilrush on 7, 8, 9 and 10 September 1932' (National Archives, Bishop Street, Dublin), 15 September 1932

Neligan, D., 'Irregular Papers Implicating Superintendent Geary', from Chief Superintendent Neligan to Commissioner Eoin O'Duffy, Department of Taoiseach, Ref. CS 270/28, 20 June 1928, Geary files, Garda Museum, Dublin Castle

Neligan, D., Statement to the Department of Justice, Geary file, Department of Taoiseach, 14 October 1972

O'Duffy, E., 'Alleged Treachery – Supt. Geary, Kilrush', Report to the Secretary of the Department of Justice, Office of the Taoiseach, 20 June 1928

O'Duffy, E., Letter to the Department of Justice, Department of Justice, 9 November 1928

NEWSPAPER ARTICLES

Brady, C., 'Leading article', *The Irish Times*, 13 April 1999

'Leading article: Fair Play at Last', *The Irish Times*, 23 April 1999

'Shooting outrage!', *Saturday Record*, 3 April 1926

'Soon after he requested a solicitor he was sacked without any charges, a hearing or a trial', *The Irish Times*, 27 February 1999

Walsh, D., 'Superintendent's dismissal clearly invalid', *The Irish Times*, 23 January 1999

Ward, M., 'Former garda says he was unfairly sacked in 1928 on the IRA's word', *The Irish Times*, 27 February 1999

Ward, M., 'Linked hands recall Geary's fight for justice', *The Irish Times*, 17 November 1999

Ward, M., 'Seventy years trying to clear his name', *The Irish Times*, 23 January 1999

SECONDARY SOURCES

Brady, C., *Guardians of the Peace* (2nd edn, Prendeville Publishing, London, 2000)

Colvert, B. K. & Colgan, K., 'Appreciations: William Geary: 28th February 1899–14th October 2004', *IPA Journal*, December 2004, pp. 130–1

Coogan, T. P., *The IRA* (Palgrave Macmillan, London, 2002)

Fennelly, T., *Fitz* (Arderin Publishing Company in conjunction with the *Leinster Express*, Kildare, 1997)

Garda Síochána (Discipline) Regulations 1926 (Government Publications, Molesworth Street, Dublin 2)

Garda Review, February 1927

Geary, W., 'Letter', *IPA Journal*, February 2003, p. 73

Leahy, T., *Memoirs of a Garda Superintendent* (Hero Press, Kilrush, 1996)

Macardle, D., *Tragedies of Kerry 1922–1923* (10th edn, Irish Book Bureau, Dublin, 1924)

Mahon, T. & Gillogly, J., *Decoding the IRA* (Mercier Press, Cork, 2008)

McGarry, F., *Eoin O'Duffy: A Self-Made Hero* (Oxford University Press, Oxford, 2005)

Neligan, D., *The Spy in the Castle*, (Gill & Macmillan, Dublin, 1968)

O'Duffy, E., *General Order 1922*, 21 November 1922, Garda Museum, Dublin

O'Malley, E., *Army without Banners: Adventures of an Irish Volunteer* (Houghton Mifflin Company, Boston, 1937)

Ryan, M., *Liam Lynch – The Real Chief* (Mercier Press, Cork and Dublin, 1986)

INDEX

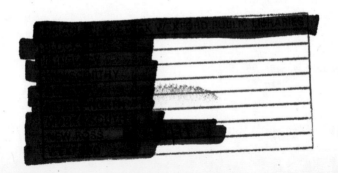